Out of the Box Owl
Not Your Basic Pitch Marketing

Mary Shannon Moore

Creative Online Strategies for Success-Driven
Real Estate Agents and Entrepreneurs

Acknowledgment

This book is dedicated to my best friend Nancy. She has been there for me through thick and thin and stood right by my side. She's my rock and a huge inspiration. Nancy is what's right about the world.

I also dedicate this book to Mr. Noah Mandel, who passed away too soon. I finally finished the book! Better late than never.

Special thanks to Bob Garagliano for all the editing help. I think you missed your calling.

Why did I write this book?

I'm going to tell you my story and how I got into real estate.

I lived a pretty privileged life on an island and had almost anything I needed or could ask for, until I turned 13. That's when my parents got divorced. My father got remarried shortly after the divorce and my mom hooked up with a young guy neither of their significant others wanted to deal with kids.

My brother tried to shoot my mom's boyfriend. He was sentenced to a live in drug rehab. Neither of my parents really wanted the kids around and their insurance paid for the program, so I was brought to live there as well when I was 13. Even though I had not done any drugs. To say it was traumatic is an understatement. They took everything away from you- no TV, no radio, no razors, no calendars no nothing and that's just the beginning. You were walked to the bathroom and watched 24/7. At night you were locked in your room and in the day you listened from 7am-9pm to people who used drugs and what they were going to do to change. People sat at the doors so no one escaped. The schooling was limited and I didn't go to most of middle school or high school.

In my later teens I ran from the program, hitchhiked to NY and stayed with a family friend. The father had been in a similar program when he was in his teens. He called my parents and convinced them to take me out of the program prior to me turning 18. They couldn't keep me at their house for long so I got a job at a local sandwich shop and I rented an outdoor screened lanai/porch from a friend.

I'll admit, I got a little wild and ended up pregnant by the time is was 19. I was still living on the porch when I found out I was pregnant. Her father and I saved up enough money to get a small home. It happened to be infested with termites but we didn't care because it was right on the beach and only $500/mo in rent. Things didn't work out with him and I left him when she was 3.

Single with a young child and no education, I needed to figure out my life.

I took a class and got my GED and began working at the local jail. When I moved out I was 50 miles one way from my job. I sucked it up and made the best of it. At least I had a steady job to support my child.

I met my current husband and we moved in together and had another girl. While pregnant with her I became violently ill and had to quit my job at the jail. I began to buy men's suits from Salvation Army and Goodwill for a few bucks and resell them for over $100 on EBay. I was able to do that and stay home with my girls.

In 2004 we were expecting our third child. I wanted each of them to have their own bedroom and the home we were living in at the time was around 1000 sq ft. I knew I didn't have much of an education and we didn't have much money. I began to look at jobs where I could use my expertise of the area and my love of marketing. I decided I wanted to be a real estate agent. I told my husband that I was going to school to get my RE license. I was 9 months pregnant and due to deliver the baby at the end of July. My husband thought it was a crazy idea and I was just a psycho pregnant lady. I told him that I was going to make double his salary by this time next year. He rolled his eyes.

I got my RE license on July 12, 2004. My baby girl was born on July 29, 2004. She was very sick when she was born. Two weeks later on Friday, August 13, 2004 Hurricane Charley hit my town and ripped it apart. I started to think I made a big mistake choosing this line of work.

I spent a two weeks with my new baby and devised a plan. I was going to be the investor specialist. I was going to help put my town back together. I went out and began looking at the hurricane damaged homes that were hitting the market. People/investors were stopping in front of these homes asking questions. I was there to answer them. I began to make connections in the community and started to make a name for myself. My first year in RE I sold $10 million in hurricane damaged homes all under $100k. I brought my baby with my to evaluate the homes. I made 5 times what my husband made- my first year in RE. I made it work. It wasn't easy, I worked long hours but I did it.

I homeschooled all three of my girls while working as a full time Realtor. I brought them with me when I had to. I had to succeed and show my girls I could do it.

In January 2010 I opened my own brokerage and at the end of last year I open my construction company.

I now live on the very same island I did when I was 13. I own 10 rentals, have two businesses, three fantastic girls and two really cool dogs and a husband who's supportive. Things are pretty good these days, for the most part.

Trust me, it's not always rosy, even today. There are days that completely suck and things that go wrong but I know that I can deal with it and work through it.

One of the reasons I wrote this book is because I know what it's like to be on your own and not have the answers and be scared and discouraged. I'm here for each and every one of you. If you feel that way, reach out to me and I'll do my very best to help you out and give advice.

That's my story. It's not easy, it's not pretty and it was hard but I did it. I figured out how to make it work and you can too!

About the Author

Mary Shannon Moore is a dedicated and highly successful real estate professional, social media leader, national public speaker and published author. She was born and raised in southwest Florida and began her career in real estate twelve years ago. Since then, she has leveraged superior sales, relationship building, and closing skills to become a leading REALTORS® and Broker. She has combined these skills, as well as incredible knowledge of the intricacies of the housing market, to build and operate her own brokerage in southwest Florida.

Shannon has been featured in The New York Times several times, having several stories written about her and her successes as a REALTORS®, marketer, mother, and author.

Shannon's daughter has seen national and international acclaim as America's Youngest Landlord, after being taught by her mother how to invest in homes and property at the age of just 14. Willow has been featured on hundreds of news outlets, both nationally and internationally, and has been interviewed on multiple occasions on famous programs such as: The Ellen Show, CNN, Fox Business, NPR, Inside Edition, and many more.

Currently, Shannon manages her brokerage firm while also writing books teaching the world about marketing. Her goal is to impart the very knowledge that has made her and her daughter a success to real estate agents and investors. Additionally, she curates a Facebook group called, Real Estate-Out of the Box Owl, with 25,000 members. The Facebook group focuses on teaching REALTORS® how to market and we share other ideas and tips. She lives with her family in Florida.

Disclaimer

Table of Contents

INTRODUCTION

Why Online Marketing For Your
Real Estate Business?

Real estate is all about relationships. And there is no better way to reach out to people than through online marketing. Social media platforms allow you to stay connected with potential and current clients around the clock. People check their social media accounts an average of seventeen times each day, giving you more opportunities than ever before to build a lasting and lucrative relationship.

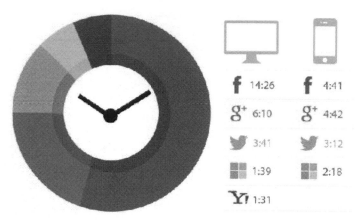

I've spent years in the real estate business. In fact, my team of investors and I have made millions using my proven marketing plan. And you can do the same. This book will enhance your understanding of online marketing and drive home why it is essential that you use social media to promote your business.

I'll start by explaining the essentials of the most popular social media platforms and how you can use each one to connect with clients and grow your prospect list online. Then I'll give you step-by-step instructions on how to engage and, more importantly, convert new leads with just a few simple clicks of the mouse. But don't think you'll get to hide behind your laptop all day. You'll also learn how to leverage in-person relationships to create win-win opportunities for you and your favorite local businesses. You'll get a glimpse of current online marketing trends and learn strategies and tactics that will ensure your business will flourish.

We all know the real estate business is extremely competitive. If you want to be one of the front-runners, you need to use these strategies and tactics effectively to gain an edge over your competitors. Success will not come easily if you sit back and let other businesses take all the glory.

Take control of your destiny by creating a robust marketing plan that reflects who you are and convinces clients to work with you when buying or selling their next home. Ready to get started?

PART I
GETTING STARTED

Chapter 1: Why You Need To Promote Your
Real Estate Business Online

Real estate is a thriving business and, with home sales throughout the country continuing to grow each year, it's a great time to be an agent. But with that growth comes greater competition. So, as an agent, you must utilize all your resources to stay ahead.

It is becoming increasingly difficult for real estate agents to reach their target audience via traditional marketing methods such as print

Unsurprisingly, the internet is now the main source for people to search for homes (92%) and real estate agents (88%)

advertising, flyers and brochures. In fact, a whopping 92% of people use the Internet for their home search! What does that mean for you as a real estate agent? Basically, if you're not online, you're not relevant. 56% of the industry's advertising expenses go to online advertising. This means your competition is online. But I'll let you in on a secret. You don't actually need to spend a ton of money online to get awesome leads through the Internet. What you do need is a lot of effort and consistency— but then you're an agent, so you already know how to hustle, right?

Marketing your real estate business online is the 21st century formula for success. Internet marketing helps build and maintain relationships with your target audience. You'll also significantly expand your potential customer base when you develop a comprehensive online strategy. Still not convinced? Here are some reasons you should promote your real estate business online:

Build Your
Brand and Business

We all know that nowadays if someone has a question, the Internet is one of the first places they go for answers. Promoting your real estate business online will enable you to create a strong online presence, especially on social media, where everyone seeks advice, guidance and reviews. When you keep your target audience and potential prospects up to date on your brand and real estate opportunities, you become an online thought leader.

Online you can tell potential customers all about your brand and demonstrate why your services are superior to those of the competition. You can convince them to choose you.

Enhance Your Credibility and Demonstrate
Your Trustworthiness

Buying and selling a home can be extremely emotional for clients, so they want a real estate agent they personally connect with. Social media marketing allows you to regularly connect with potential clients. It allows you to reveal your personality while positioning yourself as the local expert not only in real estate but in all things in your region. It's important to be an expert on so many things because clients aren't just looking for a house—they're looking for a lifestyle.

Also, social media is an excellent way to give your clients great service. By communicating in a timely and thoughtful manner, you'll increase the number of satisfied clients. Satisfying customers is the key to retaining them so that they become repeat customers.

Build Networking and
Relationship Opportunities

The Internet provides a great number of opportunities to create and build on relationships with your client base. After a customer has utilized your services, you traditionally start a long-term relationship with them by sending a follow-up email and a thank-you letter. Social networking sites make relationship building easier than ever, allowing you to reach out on a regular basis without seeming aggressive. When you engage past clients through social media, you stay on their radar and they remember you when they need a real estate agent or have a friend who does. You can also keep an eye on your competitors, monitoring the extent to which they are gaining the attention of clients, making sure you stay one step ahead of them at all times.

Reach Customers
Far and Wide

Promoting your real estate business online helps you overcome the barrier created by distance, a barrier you probably would be unable to overcome otherwise. Potential clients might be looking to move to your area and can get in touch with you online. But they won't find you if you don't have a strong online presence. The more you market your business, the more successful you will be at obtaining a deep pool of clients. Gone are the days of print newspaper ads and hand written letter campaigns. Now you can reach thousands of potential clients across the nation with just a few clicks of the mouse!

Minimize
Advertising Costs

Online marketing lets you expand your reach without breaking the bank. I don't spend more than $200 on most of my social media ads, but they are much more effective than traditional alternatives such as print ads and television and radio commercials. If you want the best return on your investment, online is definitely the way to go.

In fact, most of the techniques you'll learn about in this book are absolutely free, which is particularly beneficial if you're just starting out, don't have a huge marketing budget or both. Through online marketing, you not only advertise to tons of people. You also get the opportunity to engage with your audience, learn their preferences and receive their feedback. This makes your business stronger and stronger.

Take Advantage of the
Convenience Factor

When you market your business on the Internet, it's as if you are available around the clock. Your social media profiles and your company's website, all of which current and potential clients can browse when it is convenient for them, have no opening and closing hours. Clients don't have to wait for a meeting with you to learn about the services you offer. When they do need to meet with you, they can book an appointment online. The convenience made possible by the Internet reduces the number of inconvenient phone calls you receive during "off" hours. (Then again do we even have "off" hours as REALTORS®?)

Boost Sales Through
Engagement

Engaging with clients on social media can boost sales. How so? Your prospective clients are more likely to become profitable customers if you respond to their queries and needs promptly. Being friendly and responsive also gives you a chance to beat out the competition. Clients want to know that their agent has their back. If you're helpful from the get-go, they are more likely to trust you during every step of the buying or selling process.

What you learn through social media about your customers' preferences enables you to tailor your services to fit their needs and expectations. Once they realize you provide exactly what they are looking for, they are more likely to become loyal clients. What's more, there is a greater chance they will spread the word about your quality services.

Enhanced Search Engine
Ranking and Website Traffic

Social media plays an important role in driving traffic to your website. That means that the more social media channels you're on, the more impact you'll have on search engines like Google. This automatically sends more people to your business website. The effects of this really become exponential. When your website traffic receives a boost, you then get listed higher on search engine rankings, allowing more people to discover you when they are searching for REALTORS® in your area.

Ready to
Get Started?

Now that you understand *why* promoting your business online is vital, it's time to learn all the different ways you can go about doing so. This book is full of helpful tips, detailed tutorials, and my own personal success stories. I suggest reading through it once to find out which online channels resonate best with you, then picking one thing to get started with and doing it really well. Remember: building a loyal client list is a marathon, not a sprint. So give yourself enough time to become consistent with your online marketing strategy so that you can develop quality, lasting relationships with your clients.

Chapter 2: Choosing Your Platform
Social Media 101

Social media is the most effective way to connect with clients and prospects online. Not only that, it's free! And once you get your accounts set up, I think you'll find that it's actually a lot of fun to interact with people online and build relationships with them. In this chapter, I'll touch on each of the most popular social media platforms and discuss how to incorporate them into your online marketing strategy. We'll go into more detail later in the book, but this section gives you a general overview so you'll understand how to get started.

Before You Start
Tools To Get More Business

"Why don't I have more business? I'm everywhere! I'm on the internet, all over social media, always in my farm area, networking 24/7 – but where are the calls? Where are the leads? I should be getting more than this. It makes no sense!"

Does this sound like you? I understand your frustration but you can make things a lot easier by asking yourself one simple question. This is the question I constantly ask myself in order to keep my business speeding along:

What is your message
To The World?

Message means a lot of things to different people. It goes by many names. Some call it a mission statement, a biography, a USP (Unique Selling Proposition). But they all have the same aim: to get the world of consumers to think of you in a favorable way.

Here's a really scary question:
Are you even in control of your message?

There's an easy way to find out. Go online and check. Do it today. In fact, do it right now. You might know what your message is. But people looking to buy and sell might see something completely different when they find you online.

Go online and put yourself in the consumer's shoes. Find out the following about your business:

- What is your specialty?
- What area do you service?
- Who do you help in this world?
- How do you bring value to consumers?
- How are you different from other REALTORS®?
- How are your connections with others presented?

Was it easy to find the answers to those questions? Were the answers the ones you want the world to see? Once you've done this, you can figure out the answers to two big questions:

- Who would use my services?
- Why would they use my services?

You've really got to dig deep and know <u>how</u> people will benefit from using you as opposed to another REALTOR®. Then, once you know how, you've got to show that online. So let's look at how to do that.

The following suggestions are the absolute basics you need to take care of when starting your business. These are also the things you need to do first when you reinvent yourself or target a new market.

The 2 Must-Do Tasks When Starting Out

Number 1: Yelp

Go to Yelp.com and scroll down to the bottom where it says, "Claim your Business Page".

Put in your details and Yelp will send you an email to confirm.

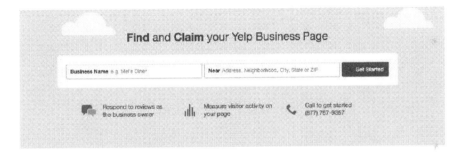

Then you can edit your information and ask your previous clients to review you. Aim to get 10-15 5-star reviews because this will push you to the top of Google. You'll then get random buyers calling you based on the review. More hot leads and we're only on the basics!

Number 2: Google My Business

Go to Google.com/mybusiness and click the "Get on Google" button.

This will take you to a page where you can add your business.

Why is this good? Well, for one, when buyers and sellers are on Google Maps and looking in your area, your business will appear with a star on the map. It will show your business name, contact details, and reviews. Before you know it, you'll start getting more calls.

Make sure you are officially verified. Google will mail you a card with a unique code. All you have to do is enter that code and your business will have even more credibility. Let me tell you, no one is doing this. Take advantage of that fact and set yourself apart.

Do those two tasks before you do anything else. Add your business to Yelp and Google My Business and you will start to get more calls from these two things alone.

Once you've done that, here are four more suggestions to help you when starting out:

1. Download Pagemodo

Sign up at pagemodo.com and download the app to your phone. This will help you schedule all of your social posts (e.g. Facebook, Twitter). I recommend you try out the free account. Once you've seen how much easier it makes your life, go for the cheapest paid monthly version. You're going to be posting regularly once you've read this book all the way through, so you definitely want to grab Pagemodo.

2. Make A Template Of Everything (Except Social Media)

Create your mission statement, core values, company statement and personal biography. If you've already done that, go over it and make sure it says exactly what you want it to say. You might even consider working with a professional on this.

You want to make a template of who you are so you can use it across multiple platforms for consistency. Make a statement that exemplifies who you are and what you do. Make sure that you feel great about your statement and that it aligns with your values. This is your go-to statement that you can keep in a file and quickly paste into different places online. When people see that your brand is strong and consistent, you will stick in their minds.

Here are examples of sites where you can use the same biography and mission statement:

- Yelp
- Facebook
- LinkedIn
- Twitter
- Instagram
- ActiveRain
- Realtor.com
- Zillow
- Trulia
- Homes.com
- About.me
- Google My Business
- Business Facebook Pages

3. Collect Your Keywords

I highly recommend you have a folder on your computer desktop for storing all of your stuff. You want to easily grab your bio and mission statement whenever you need it.

You should also keep a separate Word document that contains all of the keywords for the areas you service. You can find this by checking out the related searches on Google.

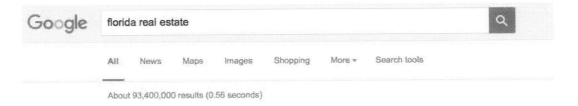

For example, if you type 'Florida real estate' into Google, you'll see related searches at the bottom of the page.

Searches related to florida real estate

florida real estate **for sale**	florida real estate **license**
florida real estate **for sale foreclosure**	florida real estate **auctions**
florida real estate **market**	florida real estate **commission**
florida real estate **agents**	florida real estate **taxes**

Those are your keywords!

Click any one of those keywords and you'll find even more. For example, look what happens when I click 'Florida real estate for sale'.

Searches related to florida real estate for sale

houses for sale florida	**houses** for sale in florida **with pool**
realestate for sale in florida	**cheap houses** for sale in florida
houses for **sell** in florida	**houses in** florida for **rent**
homes for **sell** in florida	florida **waterfront** real estate

Now we're really starting to get a picture of what people are searching for. We can keep clicking and getting more and more commonly searched keywords.

These keywords can help you to think about what posts to write on social media. They can be included as phrases in the body of posts. You can also include a set of keywords for the areas you service in the description boxes on sites like YouTube.

Keeping a copy and paste file of keywords will save you lots of time and you can be assured that people will find you with greater ease.

4. Videos And Reviews

Any REALTORS® not making videos and posting reviews is highly likely to be one of the 900,000 REALTORS® making 50k or less. YouTube is the second largest search engine in the world (after Google). If you don't have a presence there, you're missing out on a lot.

Don't be camera shy. There are plenty of options to take advantage of YouTube. The videos don't have to be long. They could just be 30-second, bite-sized clips of you showing properties or clients giving reviews. Once you've figured out YouTube (more tips further in the book), you should consider opening a Vimeo account too for the international buyers and sellers that can't access YouTube.

Chapter Checklist

- Have you claimed your business on Yelp?
- Have you registered on Google My Business?
- Have you downloaded Pagemodo?
- Have you made templates of your mission statement, biography and everything that needs to be consistent across platforms?
- Have you collected your keywords?
- Have you investigated YouTube and video reviews?

Facebook

Unless you've been living under a rock for the past few years, you know that Facebook is the most popular social networking site and almost everyone has an account. But did you know that 93% of all social media traffic comes from Facebook? This means that if you're going to be online, you need to be on Facebook. There are so many incredible ways to grow your audience through the site, which is why I've devoted several chapters to this one channel.

Facebook allows you to provide an attractive mix of content and visuals to appeal to your clients. It's not just about posting property listings, though — you have to keep in mind the 80/20 rule: provide 80% informational content, and just 20% advertising. You'll hear me say this a lot throughout the book because it's so important in maintaining your client list. If you try to sell too much, you'll lose your audience.

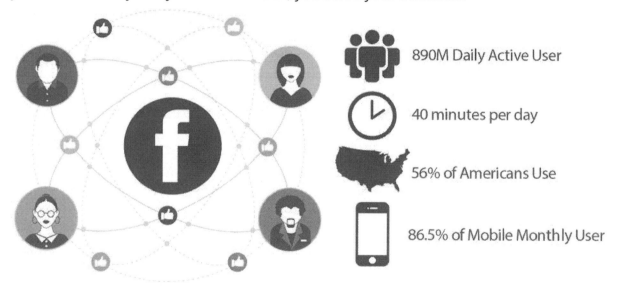

Images and videos posted on Facebook receive more likes and shares than text-only content. Put this information to good use. Post photos and visuals of attractive houses and write about their emotional appeal. Post images of famous attractions in your selling area, activities the places offer, the weather, community gatherings and so on. Strive to make a human connection through your content. If it doesn't add value to someone's day, don't post it. Interesting posts stimulate people's curiosity and those looking to buy can familiarize themselves with the place and grow assured that it and its community are perfect for them.

Facebook offers numerous opportunities to its users, including real estate agents. Most of my ideas pertaining to Facebook are free, but you can also use paid ads to target a specific audience. An audience can be targeted by keywords, age, relationship status and location.

Google+

Google+, which makes use of your Gmail ID, allows you to organize your contacts into different circles, or groups, and share different content with each. For example, one circle can be for friends and another can be for work colleagues. As a REALTORS®, you can create a circle of your buyers, sellers and potential clients. Because this platform is owned and operated by Google, the content you share on it will receive a good organic search ranking. Although it has only about 300 million active users— compared to Facebook's 1.59 billion — Google+ is still worthwhile because of the search engine optimization factor.

Those who follow you while logged in using Google+ can view your content each time they conduct a search. This is one of the biggest incentives to create and use your account to promote your real estate business on Google+.

The SEO aspect of Google+ is quite bright but, as with any other social media site, you need to keep the content engaging and relevant to your audience. You can easily post the same content on both social media sites so it's not a ton of extra work to grow both audiences. Using Google+ is free for all business owners and allows people with a thousand or more followers to make use of Google+ Post ads. Outside of your brokerage, if your real estate office has a physical location, when you are in the process of opening up your page, select the 'Local Business or Place' option. It will have you connected to Google Maps through which, during searches, you will be shown in a format that is much more noticeable. Not a bad perk!

LinkedIn

LinkedIn is a great social media platform for crafting a detailed story line about yourself and your real estate business operations. It is also a professional platform where you can showcase your business style, experience and credibility. LinkedIn provides users with an endorsement system through which your network can endorse you for specific skills. This is great for promoting your credibility to new clients!

You can also ask your connections and customers to provide personal referrals, then choose whether or not you would like to post them. It is also a good place for you to build relationships with real estate and other industry professionals. Signing up is free and people can search for you using keywords, employment, places and the experience you've listed down in your resume once you build up your profile.

Set up your business page but ensure your personal page on LinkedIn is also filled in. Include a good introduction, an attractive summary and solid reasons people should opt for your services to buy and sell houses.

Join local groups and build your network of connections. You can showcase your level of professionalism and attract a vast amount of clients on this social media platform. Like Facebook and Google+, you can also comment on statuses and follow clients. It is also a good way of keeping track of what your competitors are up to.

If you are using applications such as WordPress, LinkedIn will pull in all of your recent blog posts so that you don't need to manually post them. It's a really convenient method for cross-posting and maximizing your reach.

Twitter

Twitter is a speedy network with rolling conversations. Every tweet has a limit of 140 characters, making effective use of micro-blogging technology. This platform is known for its optimized search feature. You can easily use Twitter to tap into conversations regarding your neighborhood, city or home town and then join in with useful and relevant responses.

You can follow others and others can follow you. Tell followers who you are, what business you run, your specialization, etc. so as to make the most of your profile. Also, insert a link to your website or blog to provide access to those interested in approaching you or wanting to know more about you. Twitter also allows you to post ads targeting users with a specific set of interests and demographics.

How Twitter Cards Work

This social media platform can help you experience richer sharing with Twitter Cards for your website or blog. Generally, when people tweet pages or posts from websites, they have only a link along with a description or headline.

If you install Twitter Card coding on your posts and pages, each time a person clicks to tweet your listing or blog, depending on the layout you choose for your Twitter Cards, you can add in images, summaries and other options to go with your link too.

To grow an active following, each time you log in to Twitter, look at the people who have shared your content and re-tweet them. You can also scan through their stream to pick articles you think will be enjoyed by your followers. To ensure success with Twitter, you have to post not only your own tweets but also those of other users too, so that you can start building connections with them. This is also a simple tactic for producing additional content.

You can follow real estate industry leaders, present and past clients, and builders and mortgage brokers you would like to build connections with.

More Tips on Using Twitter

Twitter is a great place for posting news. For example, you can tweet about new constructions coming up in the area, whether they are new residences, schools or an activity area — get creative! Also tweet about things that will highlight the benefits of residing in a local neighborhood, town or area you live in, such as beautiful places to visit, charity events you support, the kindness of people, the weather and any other topic you can think of.

Make use of hash tags so that your tweets can be viewed by your followers as well as others in search of the subject matter you are posting about. You can also stay in touch with your clients using @mentions. This means using their username with the "@" symbol so they will know you mentioned them. Thank your local merchant, or congratulate recent clients on their new home.

Also be sure to tweet questions that will encourage responses from your followers such as, "What would your dream bathroom look like? #Bathroom #newhome #daretodream" or "What is the most exciting thing when moving to a new home? #newhome #moving #superexcited."

Tweet tips and tricks related to moving and staging by posting links to helpful videos and articles to things such as making a residence more attractive during a sale tour, how a move can be hassle-free, etc. You can use sweepstakes, contests and group offers to engage with clients so that even their followers can see your tweets. You can ask for good movie descriptions in essay contests while using the local spa gift certificateas the prize or offer a free dinner certificate at a restaurant in your neighborhood for entering a photo contest. You can also use Twitter to host a sweepstakes by offering a gift certificate for home décor as a prize for viewing your open house.

Pinterest

Pinterest is a social media website where you can save, sort, upload and manage images referred to as pins. You can also do the same for other content like videos and images through collections that are referred to as pinboards. All you need to do is create an account, then create unique 'boards' based on certain topics. Its market reach is huge, with over 100 million active users every single day.

For example, you can develop a Pinterest board for a particular property with its photos showcasing the beneficial aspects of the surrounding area. This social media platform is all about visuals, so the better graphics you create, the more visitors you will have. Canva is a good site where you can create attractive visuals to upload on Pinterest.

Visuals may be important but without content they are an incomplete method of attracting customers and clients. You can make use of Pinterest to show off the visuals of your listings. You can also re-pin other people's content just like you would share someone else's post on Facebook. This grows your own pins and boards so that more people will want to follow you and have your pins come up in their feed. Set up boards regarding your lifestyle to show others who you are and what your personality is like.

Here are some pointers for you to use on Pinterest

Create boards about your passion, your hobbies, the sports you enjoy playing, the food you love to eat, the places you would like to or have already visited and the groups you are a part of. You can also add boards with your favorite inspirational quotes.

Here are some ideas for your boards that are proven to be popular:

"My Dream Home" – Dream Home boards are extremely popular on Pinterest and provide a ton of eye candy for prospective homebuyers. You will want to fill this board with beautiful, inspirational and aspirational home pictures. Imagine the sort of pictures you would find in a high-class design magazine. That's the image you're going for.

Home Décor/Home Decorating Ideas – You can put together a stunning collection of room decoration ideas taken from famous designers.

Luxury Bathrooms – You can make a themed board for any room (e.g. Dream Kitchens, Man Caves, Kid Rooms). Imagine the possibilities. You can include beautiful pictures of one of your listings' bathrooms. You could show off the natural lighting by the use of glass block and paint a picture of how great that is for when you're putting on your makeup.

Things To Do In [Your Area] – You want to build yourself up as the authority on your area and also provide valuable content. So it might be a good idea to make a board full of gorgeous images of the areas of some of your listings. You could also do a board detailing the best places to eat in your area and curate some beautiful pictures of the best dining establishments.

My Favorite Recipes – It's good to have personal boards thrown into the mix. Don't just have everything related to real estate. Show your personality and let people know who you are. Put the "real" into REALTORS®. Buyers and sellers are more likely to do business with someone they feel they can trust. Other personal board ideas include 'My Favorite Cute Animals', 'My Dream Vacations' and 'My Favorite Inspirational Quotes'.

'Homes For Sale' – Obviously, you do need to put a few boards related to your actual business. Just keep the 80/20-principle in mind and make sure that the images of your listings are as beautiful as the rest of your content.

Next set up boards regarding the areas you present in your listings. Develop boards regarding the services, shops and amenities available in your locality.

Set up boards regarding home décor to connect with interior designers. You can display attractive home décor photos and create links about how to decorate homes too. This helps to maintain connection with new clients who just bought a home and might be interested in new home design trends.

Also set up boards about your listings, but keep in mind the 80/20-rule. This is still a helpful tool so you should locate it in your first four boards so others can view them easily.

Use a Facebook Pinterest tab to cross-promote. This helps you expand your social reach. How so? By using a Pinterest tab, your Pinterest updates will show up on your Facebook page.

You can also use hashtags, contests and giveaways to expand your posting reach and connect with your market. All of this helps you create more engagement and raise more awareness among potential and current clients.

YouTube

YouTube is a social media website for video sharing and if your video goes viral, it will reach people all over the world. Don't believe me? Consider this: 1 billion people are active on YouTube, viewing a whopping 4 billion videos each and every day. So think

about the reach you can have with a simple minute-long video providing a virtual walking tour of a beautiful home to a prospective buyer in the comfort of their own home.

In addition to showcasing your listings, videos can be used to introduce you and the business you conduct. You can also embed your videos onto your own website. Aim to diversify your content here too and create videos highlighting the activities and amenities present in your locality.

You can post videos on YouTube that display the best features and attractions of your neighborhood to attract potential buyers. You can also create video contests in order to obtain some user-generated content (UGC). Let them do the work for you!

If you love being in front of the camera, consider filming yourself showing your listings as you would do in person with your clients. If that's not for you, you can make a photo slide show when you receive new listings.

If you want to promote your real estate business online, you will benefit a great deal by utilizing all that social media websites have to offer so that you can expand your client base and create more awareness about your real estate business offerings. Now that you know the basics of the major social media platforms, I'll show you how to get yourself noticed by clients on other online marketing channels.

Sell A Dream
With Instagram

As of 2015, Instagram has 400 million monthly users with 27.6% of the U.S. population using it. And all those people are on Instagram with the purpose of sharing and appreciating artistic photos.

It might cost you hundreds of thousands of dollars to put a beautiful photographic advertisement in a top magazine or newspaper. But Instagram gives you that ability, along with even greater reach and engagement, for FREE!

Property buyers are extremely visual creatures, so it makes sense to go where they are consuming visual media as long as you package your content beautifully.

Closing sales is not the name of the game when it comes to Instagram. Like I've mentioned many times already, you must always keep in mind the 80/20-rule when crafting content for your business – 80% value and shareable content, 20% selling. But with Instagram, you've really got to make sure you're giving the users what they want. They won't stick around for ads or pestering sales people. They will stick around if your content makes them say, 'Wow!'

As well as sharing beautiful and artistic pictures, you want to make use of Instagram hashtags. Remember the keywords you collected when you first started? Well now is the time to start using some of them (as long as they are relevant to the photo). Bonus points if you can make a few of them funny. For branding purposes, one of these hashtags should be your company name.

The truly amazing thing about Instagram is that it has the highest engagement rate out of all the big platforms. If you do it right, people will share and interact with your content. And if one of those people needs a REALTORS® in your area, guess who they're going to call?

Check out the comment section of Instagram pictures. You'll see people tagging their friends and talking to one another. What does this mean for you? It means that someone might see and love your pictures, then they'll link the pictures to their friend that needs to buy or sell in your area. And the more great content you put out, the more great leads you'll get.

Here are some ideas for share worthy Instagram posts:

- A beautifully shot collage of one of your properties
- Luxury/aspirational property pictures (e.g. millionaire mansions)
- Inspirational quotes (e.g. about success, life, family, love, passion)
- Funny memes about the real estate business/pop culture and trends

Before diving straight into Instagram, make sure you study the masters. Look at what real estate accounts get the most likes and shares. Find out what content people are engaging with the most. Also look at how other big brands, not necessarily in your niche, are playing the Instagram game. Check out how companies like Asos, Ben & Jerry's, Audi and Starbucks make good use of Instagram.

Once you've got a feel for the platform, here are two great ways to get people engaging with you on Instagram:

Instagram Contests

Put together a bag of goodies, or a swag bag. This can be a bag of discounts for services in your area. Then you're going to create a post detailing the chance to win the bag. Tell people that they must 'post to win'. This means that other users must post a photo to your account for the chance to win the goodies. You'll get lots of engagement and lots of cool photos you can use to create and even bigger following.

Engage With Others

Just like when you post on Facebook pages and forums, you can post in the comments section of Instagram photos. Be active in the comments section of related accounts but make sure not to spam your services. If you leave a thoughtful message on a local interior design account or photography account, for example, many people will click on your profile and, if they like your content, will start to follow you. This is why it's important to make your content valuable rather than just selling. That is how you get people to notice you and provides another opportunity for clients to discover you. And make sure you follow people too!

Put Yourself on The Map

Instagram has a "Photo Map" feature that allows you to geotag the location of the image whenever you share a picture to your profile. This is especially useful when posting images of your listing areas because people interested in buying houses there might be searching Instagram for relevant pictures to help their decision. This will also further add to your credibility as an authority on your neighborhood.

Make Beautiful Instagram Videos

Instagram is primarily a photography and picture sharing website, videos on the platform are becoming increasingly more popular. Due to the nature of Instagram, with content being uploaded from smart phones, videos often have an amateur feel, which can surprisingly do very well even for big brands. This is because it gives viewers a glimpse behind the scenes. However, I highly recommend you check out the newly released Instagram app, called Hyperlapse. This app uses time-lapse technology and image stabilization software to improve the quality of your videos. That means no more shaky camera footage that comes as a result of handheld filming. This is perfect if you want to make a quick video showing an element of your listing's neighborhood. Now you can take a drive around the neighborhood, film local points of interest and have a video that looks fantastic. You could also use Timelapse to do a quick walkthrough of your listings or show off one of your favorite rooms.

While Instagram isn't a silver bullet, it is another valuable tool in your arsenal. It is another incredibly popular online hangout where you can provide value and open yourself up to more opportunities. Make sure you have visually appealing content, engage with people on the site on a regular basis and, before you know it, you'll start getting more leads.

Chapter 3: How to Position Yourself as an Expert on

Industry Professional Sites

In fact, between 70% of buyers and 75% of sellers report that they found their real estate agent online. Make sure you get a piece of that pie! Here's how.

The Internet is full of helpful resources where potential homebuyers and sellers can search for a real estate agent. If you're not listed on these sites, you're really doing yourself a disservice. In fact, around 70% of buyers and 75% of sellers report that they found their real estate agent online. Make sure you get a piece of that pie! Here's how.

Create a Business Page

On Zillow

If you're in the real estate business, you've heard of Zillow, a user-friendly home search website and app. In 2014, Zillow and its partner website Trulia spent $65 million and $45 million respectively on their marketing campaigns. Users can search for both listings and agents on these sites, so it's crucial that you create an account.

You can create a business page on Zillow by following these simple steps:

Register

You can register on Zillow by clicking the Join button located in the top right corner of the home page. You will be required to enter your email ID along with a password. Be sure to check the box that says, "I am an industry professional."

Upload a Profile Photo

Click on to the Agent Hub, which you can find on the main menu. Then click on "Profile" and start building it by uploading your photograph. You will see an "Edit" button to click, then select the "Profile" option. Go to the "Edit Profile Information" page and upload your photo by clicking "Choose File" from the profile photo field.

Enter Your Professional Information

You have the option of adding your business name, licenses, contact information and service areas on the "Edit Profile Information" page. Be as specific as possible. You can also add links to your website and social media accounts.

Use the About Me Section to Promote Your Brand

You can promote your brand and business by sharing your story in the "About Me" section. You can click the "Edit" button located on your Profile to update this section. Keep it crisp and concise and focus on your experience to demonstrate why you are the best option for buyers and sellers.

Update Your Sales History

Adding in your past sales shows buyers and sellers the level of your activity in the local area. If you would like to update your sales history, go the Profile menu and click on "Past Sales." You'll be required to know the home's full address, price, sold date, and the side you represented during the transaction. This simple step builds your credibility with potential clients, and we all know how important that is.

Connect Your Listings to Your Profile

Finally, you need to connect your active listings to your new profile. Click on "Agent Hub" and then on "Listings" so that you can access your "My Listings" page. You can then click on one of your listings and view your new profile at the very top of the contact form, labeled as listing agent.

The Best Way to Use Zillow or Trulia

If you choose to advertise on either Zillow or Trulia, ask your lender to split the costs with you and refer some business to them. In my own experience, however, I've found my free tips and advice to be more effective than paid advertising.

Another thing I love about Trulia or Zillow is the free blogging aspect along with their Questions & Answers sections, which, by the way, are also absolutely free! Paid advertising sure is effective, but when you provide people with tips and advice that help them out, they start taking you more seriously and their trust in your strengths.

Set Up a Profile on

Realtor.com

With close to 30 million unique users each month, Realtor.com is an important place to create an account. After completing the signup process, you'll need to enter your MLS credentials and read through the terms and conditions. You will then create your profile as a real estate agent. You will be able to access your Agent Profile page by going to Set up and then Agent Profile.

Import your profile information, such as your address, logo/photo and your contact details, from either Top Producer CRM or Realtor.com. This will save you some precious time and will also ensure your branding is consistent. You can use a sample snapshot report to see the appearance of your branding before it goes live.

Next, add your contact information, including your phone numbers, your address and company name, as well as your photograph. These details will be shown in your snapshot report at the top left.

The next step is to add your website address, your email and your social media page links. Also include your company logo, which will be showcased at the top of your snapshot report. If you'd like you can add your license number and edit your disclaimer. The disclaimer will be visible in your snapshot report at the top left. Finally, choose the color theme that will best suit your snapshot report and select the check box option if you are asked to display your state/province and city.

Become The Authority
On Reddit & Quora

Reddit

Reddit calls itself 'the front page of the internet'. And with good reason. The site gets over 200 million monthly unique visitors and has extremely high engagement. If you have a question about anything – and I do mean anything – Reddit is the place to go.

Reddit is a massive content and information sharing community made up of countless smaller communities known as 'sub-reddits'. Popular sub-reddits include 'todayilearned', 'relationships', 'movies', 'aww' and 'LifeProTips'. If you go to any one of these sub-reddits, you'll find tons of conversations going on. These conversations come in the form of 'threads'. This is where people come to ask questions about all manner of things and authorities come to impart wisdom.

General real estate and related sub-reddits include:

- r/RealEstate
- r/Realtors
- r/Architecture
- r/DesignMyRoom
- r/Homeowners

You can subscribe to these sub-reddits and then answer any questions you feel you are an expert on. You should also find sub-reddits more closely targeted to your niche/area. For example, a REALTORS® in Florida would probably want to check in on r/FloridaRealEstate.

Be careful because you must be extremely cautious with what you post on Reddit. People on Reddit, known as Redditors, are very discerning. If you post anything that looks like spam or seems too self-promotional, they will be incredibly vocal about it and you could even have your account taken down. You must provide value on Reddit, not shameless self-promotion. If people love your answers and see you as an authority, they will consequently get in touch with you if they need your services.

One of Reddit's greatest features is its many AMA (Ask Me Anything) threads. This is where authorities from all industries make themselves available to answer any questions the general public might have. Movie stars, comedians, presidents, scientists, authors and many more celebrities and notable figures have done AMAs with great success. There's no reason why you can't do your own mini-AMA. If we use Willow from the case study on page 135 as an example, she could start a thread with this headline: 'I am a successful 14-year-old home flipper, ask me anything'.

Reddit has a system based on "upvotes" and "karma". It sounds complicated but it's really just a ranking system. If you provide a helpful answer to someone's question, the people on Reddit will "upvote" you, which pushes your answer to the top of the page. If you provide a bad answer, they will "downvote" you, which pushes your answer to the bottom of the page. Obviously, you want to provide good content and helpful advice because then you will appear near the top of the page and more people will see you. "Karma" is basically just points, like in a video game, and you'll get more based on how helpful you are.

Quora

Quora calls itself "the best answer to any question". This description is right on the money. If you want an in-depth answer to any question you might have from industry professionals all over the world, Quora is the place to go.

The answers on Quora are much more in-depth than those on Reddit. In fact, many of them are full-blown blog posts. You also have the ability to link up your Facebook and Google+ account, so any work you do on Quora will get shared there too and reach even more eyeballs.

Quora has topics that span across all industries. It's well worth your time to sign up and subscribe to a few of these relevant topics. I recommend subscribing to general real estate topics along with niche topics concerning just your farm areas. Once you've set your preferences, you will be confronted with questions that people need the answers to on your homepage feed. If you see a question that interests you or that you're an expert on, click on it and type out a thoughtful answer for everyone to see. Your answer will appear near the top if it gets many views, comments and upvotes.

Here are a few example questions that have appeared on my feed recently:
* Sarasota real estate agent recommendations?
* What is it like to live in Florida?
* Is buying a property in Sarasota a good investment?
* Which is a better place to live? West Palm Beach, Tampa, or Ft. Lauderdale?
* What should a person consider when moving from New York to Florida?

If you saw similar questions for your own area, I'm sure you would have more than a few informed opinions in order to adequately answer. Don't underestimate Quora. Whenever someone types a question into Google like those above, Quora gets often gets special preference and ranks highly. So potential clients are likely to find you by typing their concerns into Google, coming to Quora and then seeing your helpful and insightful answer.

How to Use Craigslist to
Generate Leads

Another great source for prospecting buyers or sellers is Craigslist. It's a free and simple tool that can bring in fantastic results. Craigslist is designed to be specific to your local city or region (depending on how large your town is) so start off by finding the CL page closest to where you live. Once you're on the page, look at the "Housing" section. There you'll find a link to "Real Estate for Sale." Click on it and you'll find tons of listings for real estate properties on the market. This is one more avenue for listing your properties to reach as many potential buyers as possible.

To get the most amount of views possible, make sure you pay attention to the keywords in your listing. Many people search CL by keywords rather than by browsing, so it's vital that you use the proper wording. Otherwise, you run the risk of your post not being found by anyone. You can either work them into the text or simply write a line at the bottom of the listing that simply says, "Keywords: North Port Real Estate, Condo For Sale," and any other relevant words or phrases. Then when someone types in any of those words into the search field, your listing automatically appears.

Next it's time to craft your headline. Make sure it's compelling and emotional so that it really grabs people's attention. Here is a list of some power words to use both in your headline and in your listing text:

- Luxurious
- Updated
- Remodel
- Spotless
- Immaculate
- Value
- Superior
- Quality

As with any listing, make sure that your accompanying photographs are professional and highlight the very best of the property. They should be bright and colorful in order

33

to really grab people's attention and stand out from the scores of other listings on Craigslist. Carefully select the best one to serve as your cover photo. Now I also have to give you a word of caution here. We all know that the Internet, and Craigslist, are full of scammers. One such method they use with real estate is to steal photographs and create their own listings. Some might do it just to mess with people, while others are trying to phish for personal and financial information from unsuspecting house hunters. To help deter people from stealing my photos, I usually stamp each picture with my contact information in the corner of the picture. It's not a foolproof method, but it does make my photos less attractive to scammers who may want to lift them to use as their own.

Now back to the listing. Craigslist now lets you input your contact information that appears in a "Reply" drop down menu to help minimize people gathering your personal contact information to use for spam. But I still also like to include my contact information in the listing text to make it as easy as possible for people. I let people know that they can call or text my cell phone, and also supply my email address. I always prefer to give people all of their options so they can contact me the way they feel most comfortable. If you created a single property website for the listing, you can also include that link so they can find out more information. Once you've posted your listing, you can repost the same one every few days so that it appears a more recent post.

Another quick tip for prospecting buyers using Craigslist is by creating a post in the Real Estate for Sale section that is looking for a specific type of home. Here's an example of some ad text. "I have a buyer looking for a 3/2 in the North Port, FL area. Do you own a home in North Port? Give me a call!" Then add in your contact information. Even if the buyer doesn't like any of the responses you receive, you might still get a listing out of the process.

Chapter 4:
Attract Out-of-Town Buyers with City-Data.com

New agents and more seasoned professionals alike can benefit from participating on a website called City-Data. It has a huge forum section where you can find information about the things people are talking about in your local city. The traffic stats at City-Data.com are pretty impressive. The site has reached 11.5 million absolute unique visitors per month with 92.2% of visitors from the US. This is a great platform to acquire new buyers but, unfortunately, most real estate agents are unaware of how to leverage its power effectively. Most of the people who discuss things on the website are the ones who are about to move into the area, so it's a spectacular place to get new client leads - if you know how.

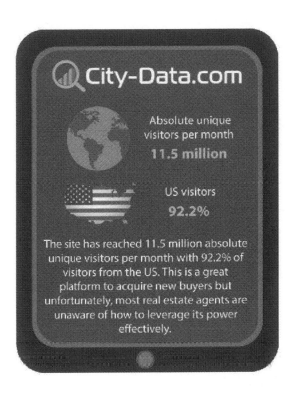

Exploring City-Data.com

I have been using this website for over 8 years and I can tell you one thing for sure. Every day, without fail, I get at least one potential buyer from this site! Yes, people, I'm talking about really excellent leads. City-Data has people moving to your area from all over the world in search of answers to their questions and solutions to their problems. Here is what you need to do to set up a page on this amazing, underutilized website:

Go to City-Data.com... Click on the tab that reads 'Forum', which you will be able to find on the top left of the page.

On the top right, in really small print, you will see a link that says 'Register.' Use it to create a username. Remember that others may form their perception of you based on your username, so think about it before you decide.

Next, you will have to choose a password, put in your email address and agree to the forum rules.

Once you're done with the steps listed above, the website will take you to a page informing you that your registration has been completed. You will then have to click on the link that says 'Profile.' Fill out your profile page and 'Save' it. There is a 'Control Panel' located on the left hand side of your page. You can use this panel to edit your profile, view and send messages, and sign up to receive alerts from certain groups, etc.

You then need to go to the US forums, or wherever you are located internationally, and find the city closest to you. The forums I post on regularly are in Florida, specifically the Punta Gorda-Port Charlotte board and the Sarasota-Bradenton-Venice area board. All you have to do is click on the link in your area. You will then see discussion threads running down the left side of the page. Here are some examples of a few that are currently on my page:

"What is life like in Bradenton?"
"North Port 55 + Gated Communities"
"Montessori/Waldorf Schools in Sarasota"
"Flood Policy Changes"
"Pool Services"
"Best Hospitals in FL"
"Moving to Sarasota Area!!"

By clicking any of these links, you will be able to view the things people are asking locals and you will be able to respond to them. Before you do, it's important to remember this rule: you may not directly solicit on this website or you will be banned immediately!

You cannot say you are a real estate agent out right or sign your name on a post. But people will know you are an agent by the little house symbol appearing beside your name and they will be able to click on your profile to get your contact information and details. In order to get this particular symbol, you can join the Real Estate Agents user group. Doing so will have your user title changed to 'Real Estate Agent', earning you the small house symbol which will then be displayed beside your name, visible on all your posts. This is why you need to properly fill out the correct information on your profile page so that people can get in touch with you.

Your potential client base will then become aware of your being a REALTORS® and can contact you or visit your website. Here's how to join the Real Estate Agents group:

Click on 'My Settings' and then 'Group Memberships' Select 'Join Group' Then make sure you select 'Identify me as a member of this group, 'which you will be able to locate next to 'Real Estate Agents' and 'Update Display Group'.

Don't underestimate how valuable this website is. Signing up is a must! I have been using this website to answer many posts and most of them aren't even related to real estate. Once you start posting frequently, people will begin to notice you, get to know you, and eventually, start trusting the things you say. You will establish yourself as a subject authority. I answer posts related to dog grooming, pools, schools, real estate and everything in between.

I have been on the City-Data website since December 2007 and it's where I get most of my business from. I currently have over 7,000 posts, over 32,000 have clicked to view my profile and my posts have been read over 17 million times.

Helpful Tips on Using
City-Data.com

If you want to find me on the City-Data website, please feel free to do so. My user name is SoFLGal. You can go to my page and study the manner in which I answer posts. You can also read through a few of the blog posts I wrote on my page to get some ideas for your own page on this website. Here are a few pointers to help you out:

Choosing a Name

Let me tell you that I wouldn't have chosen the name I currently use had I really thought this through. If I had pondered a bit more on this, I would have probably opted for something like FLNative. The reason for doing so is that it will allow people to be informed about the fact that I was born and raised in FL, automatically boosting me as an expert in my state.

Entering the Agents' Forum

After you log on to the website, go to the forum where all the real estate agents active on the website talk to one another. You can also get great ideas here for the name you want to go by.

Setting up meetings

I generally set up meet up sessions for the group. This makes for a good way of getting acquainted with each other. It will also prove to be a great way of cementing your business on this website.

Answering a Question

If I find myself in a situation where I don't know the answer to a particular question, I usually do some research before providing an answer. I do so by Googling the question and if I'm unable to find the answer, I seek help from people on other forums. I do this because I want to provide people with the correct answers so that I can help them out with whatever it is they are confused or curious about.

Here is an example. Not too long ago, someone wanted to know the height of the bridge in Punta Gorda. I did not have the answer but I did know how to obtain it. I called a well-known local expert who goes by the name "Fishin Frank." He owns a local bait shop. When I approached him, he provided me with more than enough information to enable me to answer the question.

It's not about knowing all the answers. What's more important is knowing where and how to obtain them. You can't possibly possess every ounce of knowledge that exists on this planet but you sure can obtain it from the right sources.

Making Your Interest Known

Once you've posted your answers, you can send the person who asked the question a message, but avoid doing the whole sales person thing. Let me shed some light on this by giving you an example. I may post on someone's thread by answering their query about the bridge height and then I could also send them a private message, addressing their concerns about the boat they own, that would read something like this:

"You didn't mention the size of your boat but there are also a few other areas I can recommend that might work out for you. Of course, if you have a sailboat you'll need a water way with no bridges.

Also, I'm not sure if you are aware of this, but the city of Punta Gorda pays to maintain the sea walls. Get back to me on what type of boat you have and I can get you more information."

See what I did right there? I basically gave them some more information they were not aware of but proved to be useful to them. You need to show an interest in them and provide them with some useful knowledge and facts that are relevant to the topic of discussion. Also, ask them a question so as to give them a reason for getting back to you.

Posting Your City

If the name of your town is not listed on the City-Data website, you can post in the name of the nearest listed town. This is where everybody else will be posting for your city as well.

Securing Yourself on the Website

In my opinion, the most beneficial thing to do upon joining the City-Data website is to read the Terms of Service (TOS). The TOS of City-Data is just like the one Facebook and every other forum out there has. One thing that is highly useful about their Terms of Service is that it will help you adopt certain precautionary measures that will benefit you on this website. For example, it will keep you from getting banned from the site. You can also learn more about the purpose of the forum and how best to use it.

This website is an amazing platform for meeting people and allows you to be helpful to others. All you need to know is that City-Data is kind of like a rare breed of bird and they intend on keeping it that way.

Chapter 5: Content Creates Connections

Engage Potential and Current Clients by Blogging

Have you heard of WordPress? It's a free hosting website. That's right! It's free and you can start a blog on WordPress without any cost. You can use your blog to talk about pretty much anything going on in your local community.

Let me share my own experience with you. A good percentage of my clients feel as though they know me personally because they've been following the blog posts I've written over the past ten years. Following the 80/20 rule, I've based the majority of my blog posts on random topics ranging from kayaking to gardening and have even posted about my dogs.

The reason I've done this is because my experience has taught me that the less sales talk you do, the better. Nobody likes to constantly hear about how they can buy this and why they should buy that all the time.

One thing they do like, however, is pictures. Everyone is fond of viewing photo shots. So when you write about kayaking, take a shot of the manatee and post it on your blog. When writing about your pets, post a picture everyone will fall in love with. There are plenty of animal lovers around!

When I talked about Sandhill Cranes in one of my blog posts, I posted a few shots of some I found on the side of the road in Englewood. Do you know why I did that? Because when people search for Englewood, FL, my blog will come up in the search listings. Regularly performing small actions like this one eventually add up to better organic search rankings, so be descriptive in your posts.

If you base your blog posts purely on real estate, people will eventually get bored and move on to something else. But when you start posting about interesting topics that will grab the attention of your readers and prospects, they will start following your blog posts and when they are ready to buy, they will turn to none other than you.

How to Set Up a
WordPress Blog

Now that you know the power of blogging, get started by registering your blog on WordPress. Here is what you'll need to do:

Update Your Title

You are supposed to select a URL at the time of your registration but you can choose your very own title depending on what you would like to convey to your readers.

Choose a Theme

The theme is the look of your page. You can browse free options and choose a theme that will be a perfect fit for your blog post.

Adding a Background or Header

Creating a background or a header allows you to customize your blog the way you want - for free! You can add in your favorite color or your favorite snapshot to display your personality or convey your location.

The Addition of a Favicon

As opposed to the WordPress logo, your blog icon, known as a favicon, will appear in the address bars of the visitor's browser, so you should add an image for your icon that is unique and appealing.

Adding a Widget

Widgets are basically add-ons that give your blog the ability to gain more content and functionality. There are tons of widgets you can use and they perform many different operations, from highlighting your archives all the way to displaying your Instagram photos. You can begin with a text widget, easy and simple, and add in a tiny description about your blog on the sidebar, telling visitors exactly what they can expect while there.

Creating Posts

Posting on your blog is a good way of capturing and retaining the interest of your present and potential client base. You always want to showcase your own personality and interests, but if you're stuck for ideas, here are some tips to get you started blogging:

- Gardening tips
- Tactics for cleaning your pool
- Fun activities to do, such as kayaking, golfing, or exploring the beach
- Pet stories or any fun new things your pet is doing (people love animals)
- Things to do on a nice sunny day
- Bracing for harsh weather conditions
- Best places or things in your locality or town such as parks, restaurants, nightclubs, activity centers, shopping centers or the things that attract you to these places

You can blog about anything you think you yourself would stop to read if you were browsing through the site. This will help you brain storm more interesting ideas for the blog. Once you set yourself upon this website, you need to start blogging. Keeping in mind the 80/20 rule, here are some of my blog topics:

- "How to Figure the Taxes in Sarasota County"
- "West Coast of FL vs. East Coast of FL"
- "Looking for a Historical Home in Sarasota?"
- "Questions About Buying a Condo"
- "Sarasota County Homes in the $300K range"
- "Hurricane Strike Possibilities"
- "Closing Costs When Buying a Home"
- "How Are You Represented?"
- "Lookin' for Good Ole Southern Food?"
- "Fun Florida Family Activities"
- "Interesting Florida Facts"
- "Thinking of Moving to Sarasota, FL? Here are Some Helpful Tips"
- "Little Gasparilla Island Living and Crabbing"
- "Where to Donate for the Holidays in Sarasota County"
- "Home owner's Insurance Tips"

Your blog posts will remain on your profile page, but the posts move up the page when people respond to them and down the page as new ones are added. Also, this website is extremely active and is known to generate a great deal of traffic.

Still not convinced that you should blog about a lifestyle rather than real estate? I'll give you an example. People have contacted me to purchase a home after reading about my basset hound on my blog. Why? They were searching Google for the places in Florida they would be able to buy a basset hound from and were also interested in purchasing a house in Florida.

They happened to find my blog, connected with me, flew in a few days later and purchased an $800K home from me. I've also had people contact me after stumbling upon a blog post I wrote about growing tomatoes and ended up buying a home from me. Of course, people have also contacted me about my real estate blog posts but you can widen your reach significantly with diverse content.

Create the
Perfect Blog Post

In this section, I will tell you what goes into the creation of a perfect blog post, why you need to include certain things, and the tactics through which you can get people to view your blog. I'll start by critiquing a blog post I wrote about kayaking. First, let me tell you that kayaking is huge in Florida and a great popular local spot is Lido Key.

Lots of people search for kayaking on Lido Key and a great majority of them are tourists. My thinking is that if they're here on vacation, it's possible they may also be looking to buy some property. Each time any one Googles the term "Kayaking Brushy Bayou Lido Key," there I am! And then they'll discover that I sell real estate too. If they want to buy a home, of course they are going to select the agent who understands their interests.

A major reason people move to a different location is the weather. This is why I mostly tend to mention weather in the content I post. I say things like: "Beautiful sunny day with a slight breeze." The link below is a reference to the post I wrote on CityData:

http://www.city-data.com/forum/sarasota-bradenton-venice-area/1217633-kayaking-paddle-boarding-brushy-bayou-lido.html

Keyword Usage

In my article, I also mentioned Lido Key around five times. The reason for doing so is so I can rank on Google for that particular search term. Tread carefully, though, when trying to incorporate keywords. Avoid being obnoxious by mentioning the thing you're trying to rank for around 20 to 30 times. If you do so, your blog will lose its meaning and will have one word or phrase being repeated way too many times and the readers will eventually tune out due the redundancy present in your content. On top of that, you may also receive penalties from Google for trying to rig the rankings! Always make sure your content sounds natural and conversational. When you do so, your post will contain a natural flow and will provide ease of readability to your readers.

The Content of the Blog

A blog is all about the content that goes into it. I'm always giving out tips on local activities and attractions. I base the content of my blogs on such things because I'm an expert in my area and my tips are not something people can easily obtain from other sources. Remember, it's always important to add value with your blog posts.

Another thing I do via my blogs is paint readers a mental picture of the things they can expect to see and do upon moving to Florida, such as crystal clear water, beautiful fish swimming about and clumps of coral. It gives off a feeling of one of those beautiful postcards you see of Florida, don't you think?

People are also really interested in learning about the history of the places they visit. This is why I also talk about how and why the canals were formed and I reference the well-known John Ringling. His name gets Googled quite a lot, which is why he's in my blog. People stumble upon my blog by Googling his name alone and I'm providing them with the history that surrounds the area too. I also posted some pictures of the old Ringling dredging barge and used the opportunity to mention his name again.

When you read my blog you'll notice that I talked about seeing dolphins. Why? Because everyone absolutely loves to see them. I've also shot some extremely cute pictures of raccoons and various birds. You know why I did this, right? Again, because of the great love people have for animals. And cute pictures of animals in a place people are considering as their new residence is sure to be a great hit among the targeted crowd.

Bonus Blogging Tips and Ideas

If you're really interested in blogging, here are some tips to help develop your strategy.

Tip 1

I think this works well on a WordPress blog and, at times, on a Facebook page too. I'm having both of my websites revamped and combining them into one, and also plan to incorporate my blog. This works well because Google likes WordPress and soon all of my content will be housed in one location to work together in getting ranked.

Tip 2

Pictures always heighten the interest of people and enrich a blog with color and excitement. Take pictures of anything interesting in your community. It could be spotting a dolphin while kayaking, a Sandhill Crane while showing property in Venice or even a turtle making its way across a road. Always keep your phone handy so you can snap a quick shot.

Tip 3

Be descriptive with your blog titles and include keywords. Here's an example of a great title: 'The Sandhill Cranes Have Returned to Venice, FL.' You'll rank for both Venice, FL and Sandhill Cranes.

Tip 4

Be prolific with both your posts and your comments. I have made hundreds of comments about my area and people are always telling me that they see my stuff everywhere and that it's really good. Because my visibility on the Internet is so high, people are always reading the things I write and this is also why I get a great number of leads for both buyers and sellers.

Any hot topic surrounded with hype has one certainty - it's going to be Googled by a lot of people and this will pave the way for your blog post being discovered by them online. You can add pictures or videos to it too, just like I did with my post about kayaking in Lido Key.

Even More Blog Ideas for Creating Quality Content

Blogging needs to be done consistently to gain any kind of traction, and I understand that it can be difficult to think of ideas on top of everything else you have to do. So here is a long list of topics that you can adapt for your blog or any other type of social media post. Happy blogging!

- The kid who just got 52 lobsters down at Lobster Fest in Key West
- The manatees out off the dock that are mating (add in some cool facts about manatees too)
- A local restaurant (post a mouth watering picture of their yummy food and tag the restaurant)
- The turtle you rescued at the beach
- The crazy bath tub in a house you just showed to clients
- The cute dog at the restaurant who was looking even cuter with a tie on
- The gorgeous crystal blue waters of the sandbar you so often hang out on
- How your daughter helped a turtle wandering about on a road that contained only danger for the poor little guy had he not been rescued (add in the name of your city to obtain a higher ranking)
- The great things you can discover on the sandbar
- A snook you were successful in catching while you were out fishing
- A funny picture you happened to stumble upon
- The community of another one of your happy home owners (you can also tag the community for more prominence)
- Your new client who is now an extremely happy home owner and their playful little dog named Snookums (you can add in a portion about unique dog names)
- A picture of your happy clients along with the closing gift you gave them and write about your experience
- How the sales price is hitting a continuous rise (include a few graphs to support the statistics)
- The beauty and soothing feelings of watching a sunset (snap a picture of a gorgeous sunset and post it along with your blog for added effect)
- Post a funny picture in regards to your area

- Post a picture showcasing another group of delighted homeowners in front of your office (this will show that your clients always end up happy and will also have your office on display)
- Take some of your new home owners to a business that helps you out by referring you
- Take a snap shot of your clients and tag them all along with the business that does you a favor
- Neat ideas for homeowners (for example, I use a tower rack and shower hooks on the back of a door to hang my necklaces)
- Another cool thing in your house being a chandelier you crafted that has the appearance of an octopus
- The history of your town
- An interview you conducted with someone in your town
- Re-blog a great article and comment on how well it is written or on the content present in it
- Post a picture of yourself with a home that is under contract to remind people you're a real estate agent in case they had forgotten that
- Include a picture of your business logo
- Include a snapshot of your billboard and ask people if they've noticed it out on the Inter state

So there you have it, folks! A long list of ideas for the type of things you can post on your blog. The ideas listed above are full of things people will find interesting on your page. It also adds in a flavorful variety and will surely attract more and more people to your page.

There are over 17 million people who have read my blog posts and information on a national blogging page. That, according to me, is a pretty good number. But let me tell you one thing - if your page contains everything about listings and real estate and nothing else whatsoever, I can assure you that nobody will be interested in reading it. So make the content you post as interesting as possible so that the number of people that take an interest in your page may continue to grow.

Show What You Know

With Webinars
& Google Hangouts

Hosting a webinar is yet another way to establish your authority and increase engagement with your blog and social media audience. A webinar, as the name suggests, is a web-based seminar. You can use video conferencing software to share your wisdom with people in real time. We'll be using Google Hangouts because it's free.

Webinars are extremely popular but few industry professionals are taking advantage of this. It can seem like a big, even scary, task. But don't worry. I'll show you exactly how you can set one up and give you some tips for how to structure it.

Choose An Irresistible Webinar Topic

Before we get into the technical details, let's figure out the most important thing of all: what are we going to talk about?

There are a million-and-one things constantly fighting for our attention on the internet. When you're just two clicks away from adorable dog and baby videos, you need to make sure you have something good to keep your audience's interest.

Here are two tricks to picking a great webinar topic:

Check out your most popular posts (on your blog and across social media platforms). Check out what keywords take people to your site.

These are two great sources of information because they have already proven the market's interest in a topic.

I might see that the following posts and keywords are the most popular:

- Thinking of Moving to Sarasota, FL? Here are Some Helpful Tips
- What to look for when buying a house in Florida
- Questions about buying a condo
- Moving to Sarasota area

All of those would make great webinar topics. In this case, I might title my webinar, 'Helpful Tips For Moving To Sarasota'.

Because I've already written on the topic, I have a great foundation to start from. The webinar will offer a chance for me to expand upon the knowledge I gave out in my posts. And, of course, people can ask their own unique questions and ask me to expand upon the answers even further. This is a great opportunity for me to give detailed examples, practical help and show myself as the authority on moving to Sarasota. And seeing as the audience will only be people interested in moving to Sarasota, who are they going to come to when they make their decision? If you said me, you guessed correct.

Set Up Google Hangouts On Air

There are tons of paid video conferencing options for webinars but we really don't have to spend a dime! All we need to do is set everything up with Google Hangouts on Air.

Google Hangouts on Air merges with YouTube, which means that your webinar will be streamed live from your YouTube account.

You will need to connect your Gmail account with Google+ and YouTube. These are the steps to follow:

- Start a Google+ account at plus.google.com.
- Start a YouTube channel by signing into YouTube and going to 'My Channel'.
- Link Google+ with YouTube. You do this by going to the settings icon on YouTube and clicking 'Confirm your name on YouTube'.
- Download and install the Hangouts plugin by going to tools.google.com/dlpage/hangoutplugin?hl=en
- Verify your account on YouTube in order to conduct webinars longer than 15 minutes.

Those are the technical aspects of setting up Google Hangouts. Now let's look at how your webinar can run smoothly.

Practice Makes Perfect

Obviously you're not just going to dive straight into a webinar. You want it to go well so you must practice. So you need to do a practice run.

First, you should know that there is a difference between Google Hangouts and Google Hangouts on Air. They're similar but Google Hangouts does not stream live to the internet. They are for private conversations with friends.

My suggestion is that you practice by starting a Google Hangout with a small group of friends and family so that you can get to grips with how everything works.

You can start a Hangout by going to your Google+ homepage, then go to the dropdown menu on the left of the screen and choose Hangouts. It's fairly intuitive so just play around for a while until you understand all the little tools and features. If you want your webinar to be like a presentation, you can play with the PowerPoint app on Google Drive.

Once you're comfortable with Google Hangouts, you need to learn how to set up an Event on Google+. It's really easy. All you do is go to your Google+ homepage and click 'Event' under the 'What's new with you?' box.

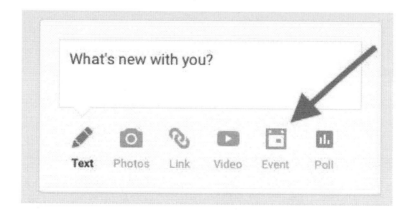

Now you want to practice conducting a Google Hangout on Air. Go to your YouTube channel, click 'Upload' and choose the 'Google+ Hangouts On Air' option.

- Here's the mini-practice process you should follow:
- Set up an 'Event' on Google+
- Send an invitation to one of your other emails
- Schedule the event for 30 minutes ahead of time
- Start the Hangout on Air from your YouTube account
- Give your Hangout on Air the same name as the event
- Get the video embed code for the video (click 'Links', then you'll see 'Video Embed') and embed the video on your WordPress blog
- Hit the 'Start Broadcast' button

That's the nitty-gritty. It will take some trial and error but it won't take too long before you're comfortable. Set aside some time to get used to it and figure everything out. You don't want to wait until you are actually giving a real webinar to discover everything.

How To Structure Your Webinar

A solid structure that you can repeat again and again with your webinars is as follows:

- 5-minute introduction: tell everyone who you are, what your story is and how you can help them.
- 20-30-minute presentation: this is the body of your webinar. If you've used popular blog posts to decide on the topic, you can simply expand that out and offer even more information.
- 10-minute Q&A: this is where you get to interact with your audience and clarify everything they need to know.

Another great idea is to end your webinar with a request. You've just given your audience a ton of valuable information, so now is the time to capitalize on that. Ask them to like your Facebook page or join your Facebook group and let them know how they can reach you if they need a REALTORS® in your area.

Be The Portable Professional With Podcasting

Podcasting is another rich area that the majority of your competitors are not exploiting. But they are missing out and there is room for you to move in. There are 46 million active podcast users in the U.S. alone and it keeps on growing.

65% of 2.3 billion podcast downloads came from a mobile device. This means that if you have your own podcast, you can talk to people and demonstrate yourself as the authority while your listeners are going about their normal lives.

People listen to podcasts while driving, at the gym, running errands and much more. If you impart wisdom straight into someone's ear, you are providing another opportunity for people to come to you. Your podcast might just be the thing to swing it for someone when they need a REALTORS® in your area.

The interesting thing about podcasting is the fact that you are highly likely to be talking directly to your target market. Facebook users might come across a post of a beautiful listing and not think much of it. But people actively search out podcasts because they already have a vested interest in the topic. If you have a podcast that gives out interior design tips, tricks for selling properties and all manner of REALTORS®-related subjects, you can be assured that the people listening already have an interest in these subjects.

To create valuable podcast content, this is the mindset shift you need to make: **think like a radio producer**.

You have the task of scheduling a radio show that has to appeal to your demographic. It has to capture their interest, entertain them, educate them and keep them coming back for more.

One of the many great things about podcasting is that, because it's an often forgotten medium, you might be surprised to find speaking to be your forte. At the very least, podcasting will give you a chance to break up the monotony that comes with writing and posting on social media.

Get The Right Sound

A lot of people scare themselves away from podcasting because they think they need to know lots of technical recording skills before they even start. This isn't true. You don't need to get too in-depth with the recording. But you do need to make sure that the podcast sounds good. Notice I didn't say great. It doesn't need million-dollar production features. But people do need to be able to hear and understand you without difficulty. For that, you'll need some reliable equipment.

The one thing you can do to make sure you have a good sound is to invest in a good microphone. I recommend one called the Yeti USB Microphone. When you're speaking, make sure you put the microphone as close to your mouth as possible. This will stop background noise from getting onto the recording. As for recording software, there's no need to spend any money. There is a program called Audacity that you can download for free.

Podcast Length

Podcasts can be a little longer than the videos you post to Facebook. People who download podcasts generally have longer attention spans than those watching clips on the internet. I recommend anywhere between 15 to 35 minutes as a good podcast length with 20 minutes being the sweet spot.

What Type Of Podcast Should You Do?

You can either make a niche podcast or cast a wider net and go for a more general audience. An example of a general podcast would be real estate. An example of a niche podcast would be real estate in your specific area. You should realize that you are not actually confined to choosing between niche or general. You can, and probably should, make more than one type of podcast. I could have three different podcasts with each of them being niche to varying degrees. For example:

- Green Lion Realty Podcast (for general real estate and business topics).
- Florida Real Estate Q&A (answering questions from interested people on social media and putting it into a podcast).
- REALTORS® Interior Design Tips (this could be more broad and focus on what I've learned in regards to design over the years).

Getting Your Podcast Out There

There are two main places I recommend you put your podcast. There's iTunes and Soundcloud. As a beginner, you might want to start off with Soundcloud first. The process of uploading a podcast is much simpler on Soundcloud than it is on iTunes. The iTunes website has in-depth guidelines to help you submit, so it shouldn't be a problem when you do want to upload there. But cut your teeth on Soundcloud first because you really just have to make an account, make a few clicks and your podcast will be available for all to hear.

Whenever you record a podcast, make sure you let people on all of your social media channels know. You can post a link to the show or show them how to download. Make sure you leave a call to action at the end of every show asking your listeners to leave a rating or review. If people have told you they have listened to your podcast, go ahead and ask them for a review too. If you don't ask, you won't get.

Chapter Checklist

Starting your blog is incredibly easy. In fact, you can do it right now with what you learned in this chapter:

- Set up your WordPress site
- Sign up on Active Rain
- Engage readers with optimized, quality content

PART II

START YOUR SOCIAL MEDIA ENGINE ON FACEBOOK

Chapter 6: Getting Started on Facebook to
Find Your Best Leads

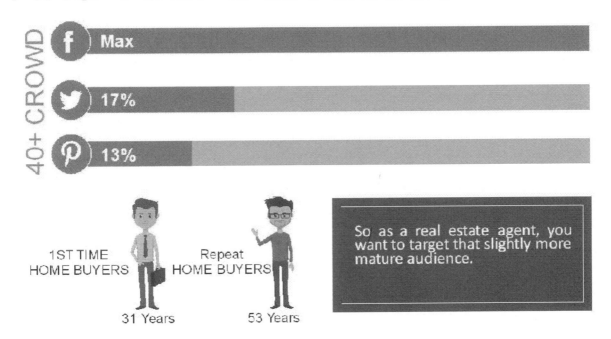

Getting Started

How to Create a Business Facebook Page

Setting up a business Facebook page is probably the most important thing you can do for your real estate business. Why? There are nearly 1.6 billion Facebook users. Now that's what I call a huge audience! And those aren't just people who signed up and never came back - those are active users. In fact, half of those people log on to Facebook every single day. Many of the younger users have made a shift onto more progressive platforms such as SnapChat, Oovoo and Twitter but none of those compare to Facebook's huge footprint. This is an automatic audience who is actively seeking fun, exciting content that they can share with friends and family. Think of yourself as a lifestyle director. It's your job to provide your audience with valuable information on things to do, places to go, and interesting ideas.

Even more encouraging about Facebook is that the 40+ crowd has been growing in great numbers in recent years and, if you ask me, this is exactly the age group I'm trying to target. 73% of Facebook users have an income of $75K or more, in comparison to just 17% of those on Twitter and 13% on Pinterest. Plus, the median age of first-time home buyers is 31 years old, and the median age for repeat buyers is 53 years old. So as a real estate agent, you want to target that slightly more mature audience. So, have I convinced you to start marketing on Facebook? Good. Now, before you begin snapping photos and planning giveaways, you need to create your Facebook business page. Here's a step-by-step guide to setting up your business page after you log in:

Select a Classification

Start by navigating to this page: https://www.facebook.com/pages/create.php. Here you will find six different classifications you can select from, such as:

- Local Business or Place
- Brand or Product
- Company, Organization, or Institution
- Cause or Community
- Entertainment
- Artist, Band, or Public Figure

The above classifications will then show you more relevant fields for your desired page. Once you select your classification, you will be required to choose an official name for your business page. Make sure it includes the phrase "real estate" —after all, that's what you do and how people will find you!

Next you'll be required to complete some of your most basic information such as the following:

The About Section

Here you will be asked to fill out a few sentences describing your company, which will then be displayed on your main page. These few lines should highlight some differentiating factors and should be appealing enough to grab the attention of your potential clients - don't be afraid to show your personality! You should include the link to your website as well.

Uploading Your Profile Picture

Your profile picture is the most important visual icon on your page and will appear in search results along with your business name and any further comments you choose to publish.

The Option of Reaching More People

Facebook gives you the option of drawing more attention to your business page by creating an advertisement. The choice is yours as to whether you would like to go ahead with it or not. You don't have to decide right at the beginning - you can always go back later and create an ad.

Adding Your Page to Favorites

To the left of your News Feed, you will be able to see a vertical navigation bar. This gives you the option of adding your business page to your favorites list, which provides easier access.

Understanding the Admin Panel

There is a 'Settings' option in the top navigation and, among many other things, you will see things like:

Page Info: Add additional details regarding your business.

Notifications: Choose to have your page customized on the basis of how and when you would like to get page alerts.

Adding Content

Facebook allows you to post content in the following manner:

- Plain text status
- Link with caption
- Location check-in
- Photo with caption
- Event page
- Video with caption

You can also add a cover photo that shows up in the form of a horizontal image spanning the top of your business Facebook page. The majority of the people who log on to Facebook do so using their phone. So it's crucial to make sure your banner and all the other things on your Facebook page are mobile friendly and that the type and graphics are not running off the edge

Expanding Your Reach with Multiple Facebook Groups

In addition to your business page, you can set up a local Facebook group or two to engage with and expand your audience. One can be for the purpose of delivering out and keeping people updated about all news pertaining to the real estate industry and another one could be for your brokerage firm.

You can add in your city and state's name with the words 'Real Estate News and Updates' or something similar so that people searching for anything related to real estate can easily find you. This is why it's best to include the phrase "real estate" in the name of the group you will create.

Remember that creating groups on Facebook is free unless you use paid advertisements, so don't be afraid to make more than one. You can include a little note at the top of the group, easily visible to the eyes of all those who visit your group. The note can read something like this: 'All are welcome to post on this group. Feel free to post your ideas, listings, articles, real estate pictures and concerns you may have. This group is home to the general public, real estate agents and anyone who happens to wander in. Grab a coffee, pull up a chair and let's chat.' Keep your text casual and always remember to sound like yourself.

Start posting on your group and keep updating it on a regular basis. Sure, the group is about real estate but you don't have to post only about real estate. Remember the 80/20 rule? Post things that will heighten the interest of your readers or something that makes them think about real estate when they stumble upon it. If you notice a particular topic or type of post engages more people, then keep pushing out that kind of content.

The main objective of the group is to:

Showcase the knowledge you possess about the area with posts about interesting articles and pictures, commenting on the concerns people have and giving them helpful advice. Since you have created the group, each time other agents post listings, pictures, open houses or articles, make sure you like them and compliment their listings. When you do so, they will be encouraged to share more posts on your group, enriching its quality and activity.

Liking and commenting on their listings will also help them in knowing who you are and will get to know you better. They may also recommend others to join the group, which will create more awareness about your real estate business and the expert knowledge you possess about the industry. This will help them view you as someone who is reliable and trust worthy and will encourage them to approach you when they are on the lookout for a contract or real estate service providers.

People will start approaching you more because of the expertise you've displayed in your advice and because of your sincerity in helping people. You will also start getting calls from agents complimenting you on your style and ideas and will put forth your recommendation when people are looking out for services pertaining to the real estate business.

One thing to note is that the group is not restricted to just agents. It is open to people from the general public who stumble onto your group, find the content interesting and start following you on Facebook by becoming members of your group. Some of them may join purely because they are seeking to buy.

So be regular with your posts but remember not to constantly advertise yourself as it will make people drift away. If you are knowledgeable, be willing to distribute that knowledge out to the masses and people will start becoming your followers and, eventually, your customers. The Facebook Group is a great idea not only to hold onto your current customers but also to bring in a sea of future prospects and leads that will soon learn to place their trust in you based on the expert advice you've been providing them. Just like in real life, developing relationships on line takes time and effort, so make sure you put in both.

How to Set Up a
Real Estate Community Group

Here's your step-by-step guide for when you're ready to make your first group. If you want to create a Facebook group, you need to go to your news feed, after which you will need to click on to 'Create Group,' located on the left hand side of the page. You will then see a pop up with the page that reads 'Group Name'.

Before randomly typing in a group name, bear in mind that your group name should be something people are most likely to type in when searching for real estate in your area. So think on this and then choose a group name you think people searching online will easily find. For example, the name of my Facebook group is 'SW Florida Real Estate News'.

Right under Group Name, you will see a link that says 'Member'. Here, you can type in the names of all of your friends you think will be interested in joining the group and start adding them one by one. Don't stop at just inviting only your friends to be members of the group, start inviting other REALTORS® to join in by becoming members as well.

I post my group page on local yard sale pages as well as general pages that include conversations about the relevant area. That's because all of those people who are members of these various pages will see my page come up on their news feed. You can also post your page on other local pages that are well-travelled. If anyone is interested in real estate in the area where I conduct my business, they will most likely join my page. It will also pop up on all of their friend's news feeds that he or she joined my group. Considering the average Facebook user has 338 friends, this simple tactic can quickly have viral results.

The next step in the process prompts you to select the 'Privacy' of your group. Putting too many restrictions on who can and cannot view your page hinders you from reaching out to the people who could become your potential clients. This is why I personally want anyone and everyone to be able to view my group and allow them to post on it. I wanted people to have to join my group to view the conversations so I chose the option "closed". Once you hit 'OK', you will be taken to another page where you will be asked to choose an icon. The icon you decide upon will be displayed right next to the name of your page.

I chose the house symbol as my icon since it is the best fit for real estate. After you press 'OK', Facebook will take you to your newly formed group. But don't stop here. If you want your page to resonate with unique appeal, you will need to personalize.

Start off by selecting a header photo to go at the top of your page. You really want this to pop because people are so attracted to strong visuals. For this, you will need to go to Google and find a photo that is royalty free and non-copyright. You can also select a photo you took that is in some way representative of the town your page features. I chose a picture displaying a soothing beach and an inviting palm tree for my page.

Basically, the picture you select needs to display a view that helps to sell your town or invite others to explore the things it offers. Before choosing a picture, think about all the reasons or attractions that pull people to live in the town where you offer your real estate services. When you know the attractions your town offers, you can select a picture that represents that and upload it by clicking on 'Upload Photo', which is located at the top of the new group page you just created.

Now you have a beautiful banner displayed across the top of your page. It's really starting to look good! But we're not done yet. After your banner is up, you need to click on 'Add a Description,' just like you did with your business page. This option lets you enlighten prospective customers about your group and why they should join. If you want a great sea of members to join your page, you need to keep it as interesting and active as you can.

One way of keeping your page active and interesting with fresh content is to invite other REALTORS® to post their listings, ideas, thoughts and advice on your page. This not only keeps your page alive with interesting content, it also establishes your name in the local real estate community. This gradually transforms you in to an authoritative figure in your area or in your real estate business and more and more people, including other agents, will become aware of you. We all know that word of mouth advertising is the gold standard in real estate, so the more you put your name out there, the further reach you'll have with prospective clients.

Get Hyper local with Subdivision and
Neighborhood Groups

Make a group on Facebook that has the name of a subdivision you want to specialize in. To get the group going, post some market statistics for the neighborhood, take some beautiful pictures highlighting it, and talk about upcoming news or events in the neighborhood. Once you have a few things posted, mail a letter out to everyone in that community inviting them to log on and partake in the Facebook page. This will help you gain a captive audience of the entire neighborhood. Try to stick more towards the informational side and place only a small amount of emphasis on the selling aspect. An example of a group name might be Englewood Isles, FL. This will also come up on Google searches when people are looking to move to the community. It's free and you can do this with as many communities as you would like to specialize in. You will be the neighborhood expert and there's a good chance sellers will reach out to you when they're looking to sell or if they know of anyone interested in buying. Another idea is to post a picture of your state and write, "Tag someone who should move (or move back) to Florida."

Post When
Your Followers Are Online

Another important part of your Facebook strategy is knowing when to post your content. Studies show that users are most active between 1 and 3p.m. Start off posting your content during these hours but confirm that this really is your peak by checking the number of people reached. You can find this information either at the bottom of the post or on the Insights section of your business page.

Not only is the time of day important, the day of the week also matters! Thursdays and Fridays are the biggest days for getting people to engage on Facebook. That means more people are liking posts, sharing, and commenting on these days. Maybe they're gearing up for the weekend, but whatever the reason, you need to take advantage of this window. Keep track of your best times for audience engagement by creating a social media calendar for yourself. Make use of the calendar to set certain days and times allotted especially for your focus to be distributed to different social media sites. Then allocate a certain amount of time and particular days on your calendar for each one of these websites, so that you can devote your attention to each one of them in order to generate more leads. You can also schedule certain posts around time sensitive events. If you know you have an open house on Sunday, post about it on Friday at 2:30 p.m. to get the best reach. Aim for 2-3 posts daily so that your message really resonates with your audience, but always make sure you're going with quality over quantity.

Chapter 7: Facebook Ad Marketing
Techniques That Engage & Convert

Find Out Who's Viewing Your Page

Before you get started with any type of advertising on Facebook, you need to understand your demographics so you can tailor your marketing specifically to them. I have so many people come to me and ask how to tell who's looking at their page so they can get an idea of what their audience looks like. Don't worry, I'm going to show you exactly how to find out!

Go to Facebook and look at your tool bar. You'll see a little lock icon and directly to the right of that, you'll see an arrow facing down. Click on that and go to "Manage Ads."

In the top left next to the Facebook icon you'll see something that says "Ads Manager". Click on that

Next, click on "Audience Insights." You'll get a pop up but just 'x' out of that.

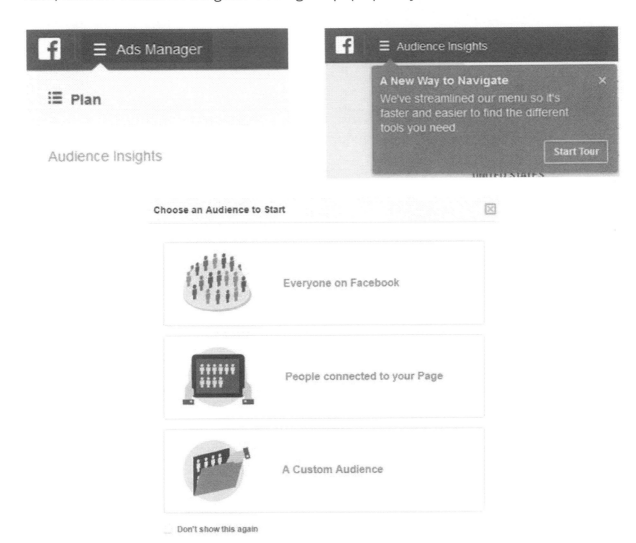

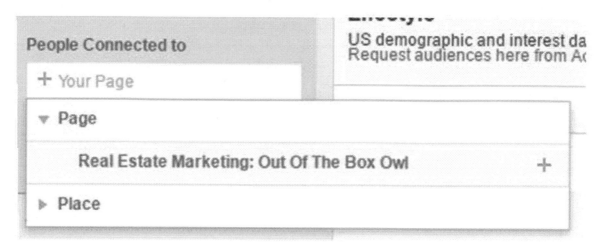

On the left hand side of the page you'll see a little box that says "People Connected To". Click that and start to type in the name of your business page and it will automatically popup. Click on it.

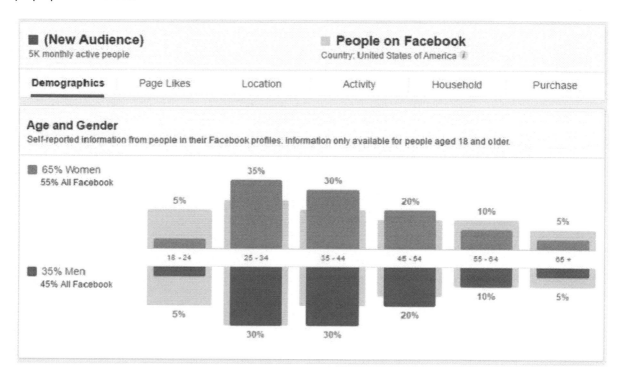

From there you'll be able to look at a lot of things on your page: demographics, page likes, location, activity, household and even purchases. So how is this information helpful? Knowing your audience helps you tailor your content to appeal directly to them.

I know that my audience is 7% less likely to own their own home than a general FB audience. This is great because now I know that my audience is mostly renters and might be buying at some point. My audience is also way more likely to live alone. Out of the home owners in my audience, most own a home valued at $100k - $200k.

Another common trait? Most of my audience has an SUV. So if I'm going to have a vehicle showing in front of my house I want it to be an SUV to connect with my audience. Additionally, many of my viewers are from New York City and Philadelphia. So I might want to target those two areas the next time I boost a post. You can tell so many things about your audience just by viewing these stats.

Once you start advertising on Facebook, you can find out who is looking at your ads to see how successful they are. This is yet another way to check your audience. Just remember that you have to have run at least one ad to view these stats.

Click on the drop down next to the lock again and go to "Manage Ads."

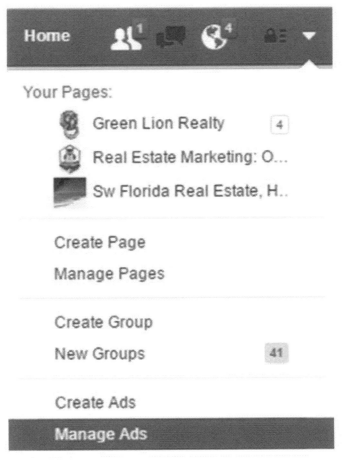

Once there, click on one of your ads (the blue link) under the heading "Campaign Name."

Next on the right you'll see a dropdown that says, "Breakdown." Click that.

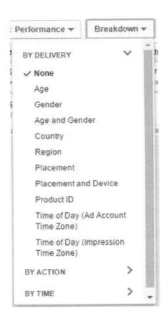

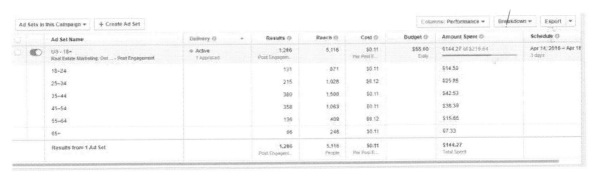

You can click on various things like age, gender, region, time of day, etc. to see specifics on a certain ad. I can tell that the majority of my audience are women aged 35 to 44. I can also see that a particular ad was viewed most from 6-7p.m. This helps you tailor your ads even more specifically in the future.

How to Create a Lookalike Audience to
Maximize Ad Impact

So you might say, how can I use this information to my benefit? By specifically targeting your ads or boosted posts to the type of people interested in your business, you're much more likely to get hot leads from your campaign. You can do this after you've hit 1,000 likes on your business page by creating a "look alike audience". So here's how to do it.

Go to back to the top of your page to "Audience Insights".

Click on "Audiences".

Click "Create Audience".

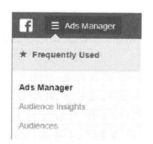

Audiences

Click "Look alike Audience".

Then under "Source" I choose "Green Lion Realty," my business page. You would select your business page. I leave the audience size at "1" , which represents 1% of the country's total population, because I want it to resemble the people who have interest within the page. Then hit "Confirm."

Facebook will analyze all its users according to their likes, demographics, interests, engagement, and behaviors most similar to the people who have been engaging with your page. For example, if most of the people who like your page like to fish, Facebook would go out and find other people who do the same. Maybe most of your audience spends $500K or more, then Facebook would find people like that.

It can take anywhere from 2-10 hours for your look alike audience to be created. You can then choose that when you boost posts and I also recommend layering your geographic area on top of this.

When it's ready it will come up in the Ads Manager under Custom Audiences.

Audiences

Go to your Ads Manager and click "Create Ad."

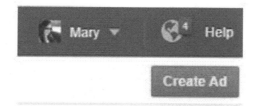

"Boost Your Post".

Then under post engagement choose your page. Pick your post you want to boost

Click "Boost Your Post."

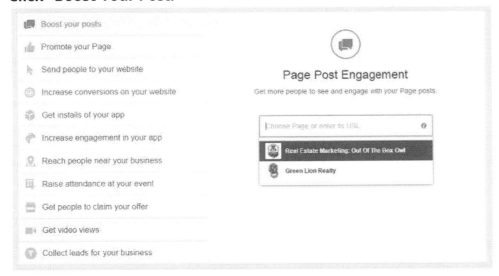

And then click "Set Audience & Budget. "

Then under "Page Post Engagement "choose your page. Pick the post you want to boost

Under "Custom Audiences" click "Create New Custom Audiences."

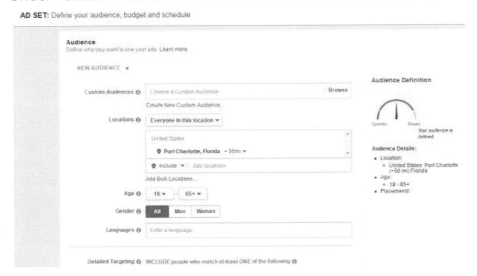

From there you can choose "Custom List" and "Upload a List" from your computer, "Copy and Paste a Custom List" or "Upload from Mailchimp". Then you "Create Audience." You can also target from your "Web site Traffic" or from "App Activity."

Grow Your Audience!
How to Promote Your Page with
Boosted Posts

If you're serious about jump- starting your real estate career through social media, then it's time to start investing in paid Facebook advertising. It's not that expensive and highly effective, making it an extremely worthy tactic for you to adopt. Let me tell you what I did. When they were having the big blizzard this winter in Boston, want to take a guess as to where my advertising was targeted? That's right, it was Boston! I wanted them to get a glimpse of our warm, sunny and inviting beaches and swaying palm trees. Do you know what followed after I paid for Facebook advertising? My phone started ringing!

There are several ways to advertise your content on Facebook. The first is through boosting posts, which adds your selected post to news feeds of people outside of your immediate sphere. This is great for growing your audience and you can base your target audience on some general demographics. For real estate agents, this is a great way to boost listings and open houses. The other option is to create an actual ad, which is posted on the right hand side of the Facebook page. You don't have to worry about spending too much on either one. In fact, you can spend as little as $5 for a boosted post and $50 for an ad. I generally spend about $50 to $100 for each boost or ad to achieve optimal results.

How to Use the Ads Manager

As a real estate agent, I usually find that using the Ads Manager to advertise select posts is the most effective advertising method. Plus, it's so easy to do. Start by going to the "Ads Manager" by clicking on the little arrow next to the lock symbol at the top right of your Facebook page.

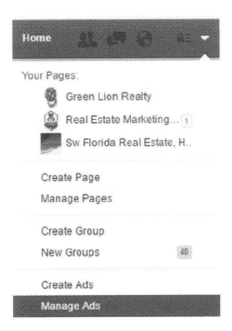

Once there, click the green button in the top right that says "Create Ad".

There are a ton of options here.

You can boost your post, promote your page, send people to your website and lots of other things. Right now I'm going to talk about boosting your post on Facebook. So click on that option.

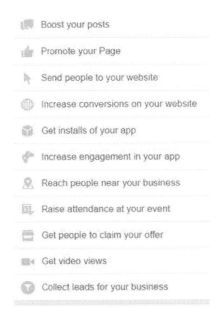

It's the first option on the page. It will take you to "Page Post Engagement". Your page will pop up in the drop down box, so click on your business page. If it doesn't, then simply enter your Facebook URL.

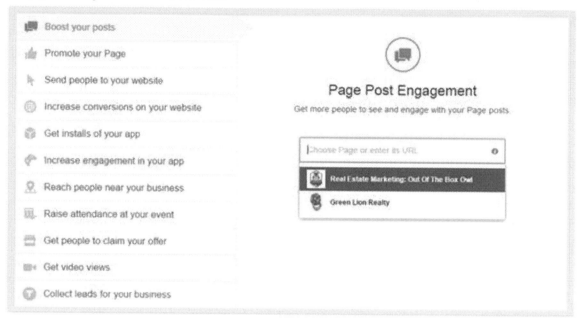

Once it populates your page in that box, it will come up with another box under that.

You can scroll through and find the post you want to advertise. It's probably going to be near the top if you just made it. Click the correct post. Then under "Campaign Name," name it something you're going to remember, such as Open House 4/16 for 123 Main St. Then in the bottom right there will be a blue button:

"Set Audience & Budget." Click that.

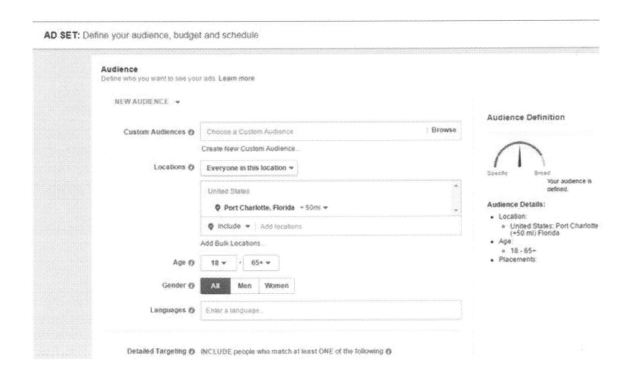

This will take you to another page. The first field is "Custom Audiences." This is where your cloned audience comes in — see how everything is coming together? So find that audience you created in this section. You don't have to have a custom audience, but if you do, this is where you'll find it. A side note- if you click to your "look alike audience," think of it as a funnel. So, it starts identifying everyone who has Facebook all over the world and mirrors your audience but you can narrow it down even further. You might want to target certain cities to keep the people in that audience in your target area. Now, if you haven't created a "look alike audience," no worries. Skip that step and leave that field blank.

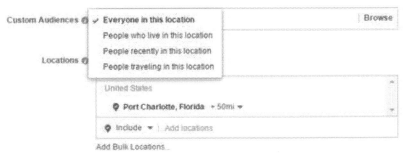

Next is location. You can choose to leave it at "Everyone in this location," which is what I usually do. Let me tell you something pretty neat though.

If you click the dropdown and choose "People traveling in this location," you can target people who don't live in the area but might just be visiting. Facebook determines this when their home is more than 25 miles away. Remember that GPS system, your phone? Facebook can go into that feature and determine your exact location. Have you ever traveled out of state and you begin to see ads on your news feed for the area you are traveling? That's because advertisers are targeting users who are visiting their area. Use this feature to your own advantage by targeting out-of-towners who might be looking for real estate.

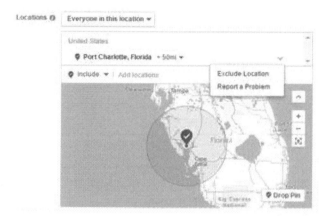

When you're in "Locations," you can choose to include or exclude certain cities, set a certain mile radius around the cities or target just the city itself, depending on your own preferred range. I usually target several cities and do a 10-mile radius around each one. It will show you on the map where you are targeting so you make sure you're hitting all the right sweet spots.

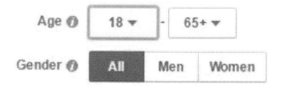

Age and gender are the next two fields. I explained earlier about how to look to see what your demographics are in your area. I generally target both females and males in the 30-65+ age range

"Detailed Targeting" is the next field. This is where it gets fun! You can break your targeting down to be unbelievably targeted. If you hit "Browse" you have demographics, interests, behaviors and even more categories.

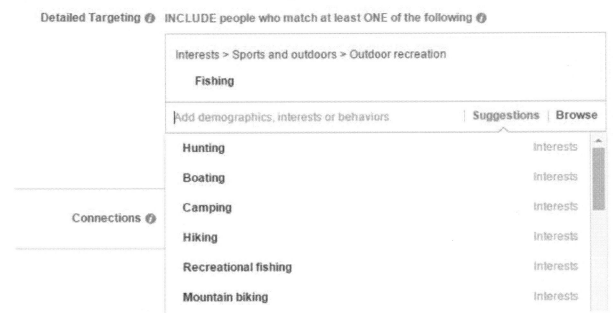

Let's say my home is on the water and I want to target people who fish. I can type the word "fishing" in the box and it will pop up. You'll see ghosted to the right of "fishing" - interests, behaviors, employers, schools and a number of other fields. Let's just click on the first one under fishing: "Interests." It comes up with boating, recreational fishing, fishing tackle, fishing lures, flyfishing, fishing rod and many other choices. Under each of those that you click will be even more additional subcategories. So, as you can see, we can get very specific. Don't be afraid to spend some extra time browsing the subcategories to create your very best target audience.

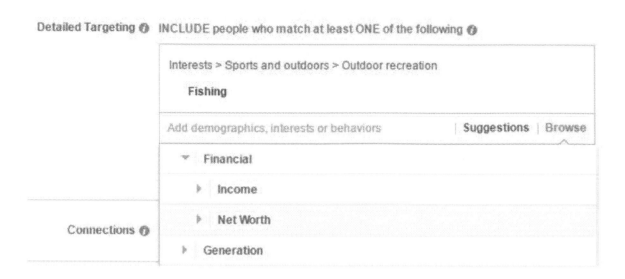

I also like to pay special attention to a few categories. Under "Demographics," I like "Income, Net Worth and Liquid Assets." Under "Generation" you could target "Baby Boomers" or "Millennials", under "Home" you might want to target "Renters" because they might be likely to move soon or perhaps "First Time Home buyers." Maybe you live by a military base and want to target veterans. You would choose "Household Composition" and "Veterans in Home." If you look at "Home" and "Life Events" you might want to target "Newlyweds". Next you could look under "Behaviors," "Financial" and "Spending Methods" and target people with several lines of credit. You could try "Behaviors," "Financial," "Residential Profile," and "Length of Residence" and target likely to move or recent mortgage borrowers.

As you can see, the targeting possibilities are limitless. Get creative and remember that you can create several ads to target all of these separate groups.

You can click to "Save this audience" if you want to use it again. Next you need to set your budget for this ad. I usually spend around $50-$200 on each ad to test it. Then pick a start and end date. I usually choose 5-7 days. For this purpose were going to leave the advanced options on the bottom set to the default.

Now you can name your ad. May be something descriptive so you immediately know what it is when you go to analyze the campaign later.

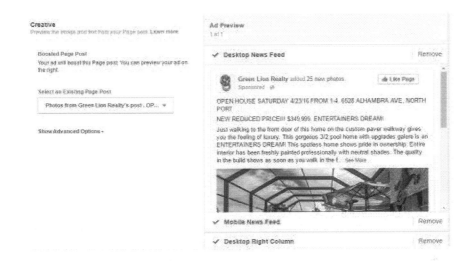

Then in the bottom right click "Choose Ad Creative."

It will take you to another page where you will see the ad on the right hand side.

If it looks good, click "Place Order."

There you have it, folks. You've just had a basic tutorial on how to boost your posts using the Ads Manager! Are you ready to create a knockout ad that will land you tons of great potential clients? Move on to the next section to find out how.

Pique Potential Clients' Interest
With Posts That Convert

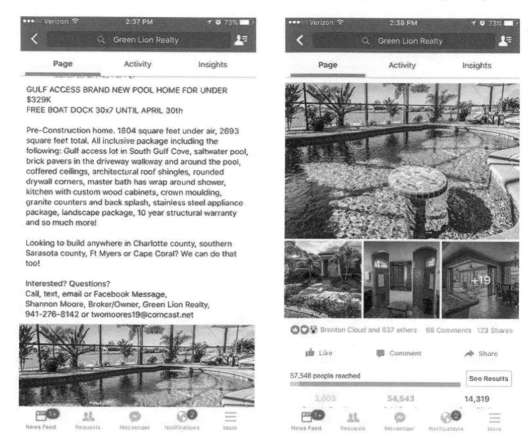

Imagine yourself sipping margaritas next to a sparkling pool in a pristine lanai. Your imagination doesn't have to do much work when the image is staring back at you from your Facebook feed. Make it that easy for potential clients with stunning photographs. This element is probably the most important part of your ad. You have about a half a second to catch someone's eye as they're scrolling through their newsfeed. Grab their attention right away by using bright, vibrant and colorful pictures, like in my example. I always recommend hiring a professional photographer to take your photos—you and your target audience will definitely notice the difference.

Next create your headline, which does a few things. It's in all caps to immediately catch the viewer's eye. This example points out a great price for a gulf-access home and I'm giving something away (a free boat dock!) and putting a deadline on it (hurry!). It makes people want to act right away to take advantage of that discount. Once you have your catchy headline written, work on the verbiage of the ad. This is the part where you need to sell the home and its best qualities. Paint a picture for your audience and make sure you emphasize its "wow" factor, like upgrades in the home or its prime location.

Here's one of my best-kept secrets that really gets people engaged with my boosted posts. Ready? I always leave out one or two key pieces of information. It might be the builder's name, the home price or the address of the property. Why? You'll find out in the next section on how to communicate through your boosted posts.

You also need to include how interested people can contact you. I always explicitly say that people can call, email or text me, then include my phone and email in the ad. I get tons of texts from clients. If you don't specifically tell them in the ad that it's ok to text, they won't, so give them the green light to do so. A lot of people are more comfortable texting than calling because it feels like a lower pressure situation. Give them as many opportunities to reach out to you at their own comfort level.

Here is another unique Facebook ad idea to try out. Make a video ad. Film your buyers standing in front of a neighborhood sign talking about why they love the area. Target the ad to current homeowners in the neighborhoods. It's imperative that you add subtitles to the bottom. Most people do not turn their sound on when watching videos. Even if the viewer's sound is turned down, they'll see their neighborhood sign on the clip and associate your name with selling local real estate. You can also send a video card with the same message to select homeowners in the area.

You can use this text as a template for your own specifics:

DO YOU OWN A HOME IN GOLDEN BEACH ON THE ISLAND OF VENICE? I HAVE A BUYER IN TOWN RIGHT NOW LOOKING TO PURCHASE A HOME THERE. Is your home 1400-2500 sq ft? At least 2 bedrooms with a den or 3 plus bedrooms? A pool would be great. The home can be in any condition. They actually like the retro look- terrazzo floors, 50s style bathrooms, funky and eclectic but are willing to look at anything in that area.

If your home is located on the following streets and you're looking to sell. I want to speak with you today!

Call, Text or email me now!

Then include all of your pertinent contact information and a list of all the streets your buyer is interested in. Even if your buyer doesn't choose one of the homes you find with this tactic, you're still casting a wide net to have leads come to you to list their home for sale.

Next let's talk about hashtags. No, we're not on Twitter, but guess what? Facebook uses hashtags, too! Did I just blow your mind? You need to make sure you are always hashtagging your ads because people use them as a way to search for things they are interested in. I generally use the neighborhood, city or state in the hashtag followed by real estate or REALTORS®. Here's an example of some of the hashtags I frequently use: #NorthPortRealtor #NorthPortRealEstate #SarasotaHomesForSale #NorthPort.

If I want to find a REALTORS® on Facebook in North Port, I might search #NorthPortRealtor. If I'm looking for a specific area I might hashtag #NorthPort. See how hashtags can help people find your posts? Think of it as having a home in the middle of the woods with no roads to it. The hashtags are building roads to your home so people can get to it.

Why You Need To
Hire A Professional Photographer

Hiring a professional photographer to take your pictures is an absolute must. Presenting the right appearance is just as important online as it is in person. You only have a split-second to make a great first impression and keep people returning to your content.

A hastily snapped iPhone picture is never going to compete with professional photography in which an expert has determined the best angles and lighting for you. You likely have put a lot of thought into what you want your brand to be and, while many of your branding ideas are likely unique, I can guarantee that you want to be seen as authoritative and professional. The easiest way to convey those two qualities in your brand is to hire a professional photographer for all of your photos.

If you need a monetary incentive, there are plenty of statistics that clearly show how professional photographed listings consistently sell for much more than listings with amateur photography.

A 2010 Redfin study found that professionally photographed homes sell for as much as $19,000 more than homes photographed by an amateur.

The study also showed that professionally photographed homes get 61% more views online.

Another study, this time from The Wall Street Journal, showed that professionally photographed homes could sell for up to $116,000 more than homes photographed by amateurs.

There are many reasons why professionally photographed homes command a higher price tag and get more attention. Here are just a few:

- Professionally photographed homes inspire people.
- Professionally photographed homes get people's attention (shiny object theory).
- Professionally photographed homes allow people to envision themselves living in the house. They can see themselves relaxing in front of the fire, preparing a tasty meal in the kitchen, getting ready in the bathroom and playing with their dog in the backyard.

Another major reason for employing a professional photographer is because you are going to be putting these photographs up on social media. And what is the whole point of social media? To get people engaging and sharing. People engage with and share beautiful and compelling content. See how this can drastically affect your bottom line?

On top of all the benefits, hiring a professional photographer is actually very cheap. In fact, hiring a professional photographer will only cost 0.09% of the median U.S. home price.

Prices will vary depending on your location. Places like New York and San Francisco, for example, will be the most expensive. Places like Montana and Wyoming will be on the cheaper end. As a general rule of thumb, you should be able to find a professional to photograph the interior and exterior of your listing for between $150 and $300.

How To Hire A Professional Photographer

Now that I've convinced you to invest in a quality photographer, you'll want to know how to actually hire one. There are a few different ways you can find one.

You can look at other Realtors' sites and see if any of them have beautiful photography of their listings. You might be surprised how few do. But if you find one that has the style of photography you want, you can always check out the photography credit and follow that to the photographer's website. Contact the photographer and see if they are available to do the photography for your listings too.

Another thing you can do is to conduct a search of real estate photography companies online and find the ones that fit your budget and needs. Two great options include obeo.com and realestatephotographers.org.

Once you've found a photographer with a good portfolio, read their reviews and see what previous clients thought of them. You could even reach out to past customers and find out what they thought of the photographer. From there, you can interview your favorite photographers and ask them about production, pricing and licensing.

How To Direct Your Photographer

A good real estate photographer isn't going to need much direction. But you will likely want to provide a list of things for him or her to focus on nonetheless just to make sure you are on the same page. Here are a few things you might wish to focus on:

- Specific interior and exterior areas.
- Amenities in and around the property.

The kitchen: is it modern or rustic? Does it have a standalone island? Does it boast spacious cabinets and countertops?

The bedrooms: is there lots of closet space? Do they let in a lot of natural light?

The living room: how can you make these look as comfortable and appealing as possible?

You can join the photographer as they take photographs of your listings or you can just let them get on with it. I think it's a good idea to accompany them while they photograph the first few listings so you can point things out and get a feel for their working style. Once you know how they work, you might consider letting them do it alone for future listings, which will give you more time to attend to other tasks.

Once they have completed the photography, make sure they are edited well and that the photographer has focused on the points you have directed them to.

Engaging Potential Clients:
How to Communicate on Ad Posts

Now that you have the perfect ad post, we're going to talk about how to respond to people who comment. When someone "likes" my ad the only thing I do is "invite" them to my page. Click on where the "likes" are on the post and near each person's name you will see a button that says "invite" if they haven't already "liked" your page. You can now invite them to your page. Once they do so they will continue to see your posts without you paying to advertise to them. This is a great, non-aggressive strategy that really works well for me.

If someone tags another person in a comment, I never do anything- I don't like the comment, I don't private message the person, I do nothing. Why? Think of it this way. If you're at a party and two people are talking and you don't know them, you probably wouldn't just go over to them and hand them your card. You'd try to build a relationship with them before doing a cold introduction. It's the same on Facebook. Plus, I've found that people who tag others are really thinking about their own tastes, but might not be looking for a home. So they tag a friend who is house hunting, even if the property doesn't meet any of their specifications.

The only time I reach out to someone directly is if they ask me a question. It might be something like: How much is the home? Where is it located? Who's the builder? Here's what I do. Remember how I said in the last section that I usually pick two things that I'm going to purposely leave out of the post? That's because I want to encourage people to contact me directly so that I can engage them in a private conversation. If it's a post for one of my builders I might leave out the builder's name and the address of the home. I do this because I don't want them going directly to the builder and also to generate interest. So if someone asked me, "Who's the builder?" I would answer on the post, "I just sent you a PM." Then I would private message them and say something like, "Hi there! Where are you looking to build? What size home are you looking for? Do you want to be on the water? What is your price range? If you can give me a little more info I can have the builder contact you." They usually respond back with the information and then I've built a relationship with them.

Alternatively, if the property isn't a new build, I might choose to leave out the price, especially if it's a little higher than the median value of the area. In this situation, I include the address if it's not one of my builder's homes. Then I answer all the questions publically within the comments, except how much the home is listed for. Once you answer something publically, chances are it probably won't get asked again. So you lose the opportunity to directly connect with potential clients.

Upping Your Ad Game
With Carousel, Canvas Ads, and FB360

Carousel Ads

If you spend any time on Facebook, you've probably seen carousel ads pop up in your own Facebook feed. Not only do people love them, they are extremely effective because they show beautiful photos and link directly to an external website. Start by clicking "Promote Your Page" just as you would with any other ad. Once you fill out your normal audience information, go to the "Ad Creative" section. Select "Edit" to get started.

Start by entering the website address of the site you want viewers to go to, like your business website, a contact form, or listing. Then type in the text you want to show in the heading of your ad. Next go to "Images" and select the plus sign to add in photos. This is a great way to show multiple pictures of a new listing or development. You can then add a headline for each card in the carousel. Wrap up by saving the carousel and clicking "Promote." That's it!

Canvas Ads

Let me tell you a quick statistic that will likely surprise you: 47% of Facebook users log in only from a mobile device. That means nearly half of all users are ONLY going to see the mobile version of any of your content. To help target this huge group of mobile users, Facebook created Canvas ads, which are specifically designed as a full-screen ad experience users can scroll through on smart phones. It also loads 10 times faster than other mobile web apps and lets you incorporate all types of media, including text, videos, carousels, products and more. The options are pretty limitless. Ready to give it a try? Let's get started.

Start by clicking "Publishing Tools" from your business page. Then select "Canvas" on the left-hand side. Click "Create" at the top of the screen and name your ad to get started. From here you'll see two parts of your screen: Components on the left side and a preview image on the right. To begin adding features, click "Add Component." Your options include: buttons, carousels, photos, text blocks, videos and product sets. You can mix and match any number of these components, but if you need some inspiration to get started, Facebook recommends starting with a theme, photo, header, and button.

Selecting a Theme basically entails choosing a background color for your Canvas. Next select a header image, such as your company logo. Once you have that fixed at the top of the page, add in the various types of content you want users to be able to scroll through. To get started, play around with videos, photos, and text. You can also insert products if you have a shop attached to your Facebook page, but this probably doesn't apply to most real estate agents. Finally, you can add a button at the end to send them to an external link like your website or a property listing.

When you have all the elements you wish to include, click "Save" in the top left corner. But before you hit "Finish," make sure you preview! Facebook will send you a preview alert to your designated smart phone so you can make sure you like how it looks. After you've done that, THEN you can hit the "Finish" button and go to your Ads Manager to set up a Canvas ad just like you would any other campaign. Once you get the hang of it, you might get hooked on making Canvas ads- they are such a fun and creative way to reach new audience members!

Facebook 360

Facebook now offers a tool called Facebook 360, which adds a three-dimensional element to users' newsfeeds. Basically it allows you to upload 360-degree videos. The user drags their mouse (or finger if they're on a smartphone) to get a panoramic view. Since this is already a popular way for real estate agents to provide a "virtual tour" of some listings, it makes sense for us to take advantage of Facebook's new feature. It's a great way to promote listings, especially for higher end properties. There's no need to purchase a pricey 360 camera.

Track Your Ads with
Your Pixel

Canvas Ads

Now that you've created exciting ads for your target audience, it's time to analyze their success and better optimize your marketing. The most relevant thing for your ad campaign is to track your conversions. You're then able to target specific offers to individuals who have already shown interest in you by visiting certain pages. In addition to tracking those conversions, you can also set up lookalike audiences to those conversions and remarket the ad. However, you will need at least 100 conversions before you can make a lookalike audience.

Get started by going to your Ads Manager and clicking "Conversion Tracking." In the top right corner, select "Create Pixel." Next you'll be prompted to select a category. If you're just creating one pixel for a campaign, it doesn't really matter which one you choose. But if you are creating a pixel to track what actions are taken through each step of your process (say, visiting your website, entering contact information, and signing up for your newsletter), you'll need to categorize each one differently.

Chapter Checklist

Understanding the basics of your Facebook marketing strategy is the most effective tool you have to reach tons of potential clients. Just like with any lead generation method in real estate, it takes time, tenacity and research to get the best results. Put as much effort into your Facebook strategy as you would with any other marketing plan you have. Here's what we learned in this chapter to get you started:

- Identify your target audience with Facebook insights
- Create effective post boosts to reach new clients
- Make "wow" factor ads with carousel ads and Canvases
- Assess your posts to further target future audiences

Chapter 8: Expanding Your Reach with.

Quality Content

Content Is King:

So What Should You Post on Facebook?

For both group and business pages:

Your Facebook business page is all set up and you understand how to analyze your audience. Cue the crickets chirping. What are you actually going to post? I often hear things like, "I have a page on Facebook but have no idea what to put on it." Start off with this general rule of thumb: I follow the 80/20 rule, meaning I always keep things 80% non-real estate related and just 20% of the content real estate related. The most important part of social media marketing is relationship building, not shoving open houses down people's throats. So keep the majority of your content valuable to your audience's every day interests, then offer some direct marketing about your business.

Here is a list of a few pages and groups I have liked or joined to get good content to share on my Facebook groups and pages. Some are National and some are local pages. Look up your city or town on Facebook to find pages that will relate to your area.

CBS News	Florida Tracks and Trails
ABC New	Florida Travel and Life
Fox News	Realty Times TV
CNN News	Florida Today
Punta Gorda & Port Charlotte New Comers	Houzz Interior Design Ideas
SWFL Kids & Family	Wall Street Journal
Dwell	Interior Design Ideas
Forbes	Women's Council of REALTORS®, Florida State Chapter
Florida Rambler	US News and World Report Sarasota Herald
Conde Nast Traveler	Tribune
Venice Area REALTORS® Tour & Listing Exchange	REALTORS® Magazine
Visit Sarasota County	Inman News
Englewood Beach Drum Circle	The Corcoran Group
Coastal Living Magazine	Charlotte County Florida Weekly

Florida's Best Beaches	Shop Local Charlotte
Suncoast Social	SWFL Real Estate Investors
Florida Design Magazine	North Port Magazine
Florida State Parks	Punta Gorda Life

Use Word Swag to
Create Unique Posts

If you look at any of my Facebook pages, you'll see that I post a lot of my own pictures and text. It looks like I hire a graphic designer, but I'll let you in on a secret: I only paid a few dollars for this awesome ability. I use an app called Word Swag and you can get it for less than $4 in the iOS App Store or Google Play Store.

When you open the app you can either take a picture to use or select one from the camera roll. On the camera roll page, you can either choose a picture you've already taken or you can use a premade background. These are great if you want your audience to concentrate on the text, but I also like taking local pictures to showcase how great my area is.

After you choose your background image, double tap the screen to change the text. From there you can enter in text or even select a quote. Once you have your text, you can get creative by selecting different colors and fonts. There are a lot of other minute design details you can go in to when you have time, like transparency and cropping. Once you like the look, you can save it and share directly on your Facebook page. I love this app because once you get the hang of it, it's so easy to make unique content.

How to Share Your Posts
On Facebook

In order to 'Share' something with your group, you first need to locate the article you want to share with others. Then click the 'Share' button which you can find beneath the article. Upon clicking this button, a window will pop up showcasing the article you've chosen to share with your group.

Located at the top left of the window is a drop down window. You need to click on the 'Share in a Group' option. After clicking on this option, you'll see a box appear in front that reads 'Group'. If you start typing in your group's name, it will appear in the box.

If you want something to be written above the article you are about to share on your group, click the sign that reads 'Say something about this'. I generally use this option to say a little something and showcase my personality. For example, if I were to share an article regarding Siesta Key Beach, I would probably add something like the following to go along with the article, adding some leverage to it:

"Siesta Key Beach ranked #1 Beach in the world!"

After you have typed in something to go along with the article, you need to click on a button, which you can find at the bottom right of the window that says 'Post.' After having done so, Facebook will inform you that your article has been successfully shared on to your page. The article you just shared will then appear on the Timeline of your brand new group.

By going to the post you just shared on the page of your newly created group, and clicking on the downward facing arrow at the top right corner of the post, you will be able to select any one of four options from a drop down menu:

- Pin
- Edit
- Delete
- Hide

'Pin Post' allows the post to stay at the very top of your page while 'Edit' will allow you to make changes pertaining to the post you've shared. If you want no one to see the post you've shared, you can select 'Hide', and the 'Delete' option, quite obviously, will delete the post you've shared.

Add Extra Value with
Personalized Content

Adding Value to Your Page

Make local community events accompanied by pictures a part of your page. You can add things like Easter egg hunts, 4th of July celebrations, Christmas parties, New Year celebrations, etc. You can also ask questions regarding the events and encourage all of your group members to start an engagement or discussion session on your page. Basically, become the go-to person on all things that are happening in your area. Remember, you're the local expert, right?

The Writer in You

If you give yourself credit for being a decent enough writer, write a bunch of things about yourself. You can also write about a certain community or an interesting place you visited. And always remember one thing: people absolutely love pictures! Visuals and graphics are more attention grabbing than text, so make sure you use them well. Actually, 87% of Facebook's most shared posts contain photos, so this is a really important component of any well-crafted post.

Post Your Property Listings

Use your page to post listings and make sure they are accompanied with excellent and eye catching pictures and descriptions. Remember not to go overboard though. Information, rather than listings, is what usually interests people more.

Engage members by asking questions about your listings such as, 'What is your opinion about the zero edge pool? I could see myself in a lounge chair with a big glass of lemonade, how about you?'

Questions like this will encourage interaction among people and help your page become more active. Also, keep the proportion of your listings less and content more. Generally, in accordance with industry standards, remember the 80/20 rule: the content you post should be based on 80% news related things and 20% sales/listings. You need to understand one thing. If people get only the hard sell and see no benefit in being a member of your page, they have the power to simply hide or 'Unfriend' you and your page completely, breaking the bond you've worked so hard to build with your potential clients.

However, it isn't usually beneficial to say things like "yes or no?" with a stock picture of some massive kitchen. I look to post things or features that are really unusual. Everyone is posting the average pictures and I think it's overdone. So set yourself apart by making your posts unique.

The Picture Guess Tactic

Start clicking pictures of various places in your community and, once you have a small collection of different locations you've taken snapshots of, play the picture guessing game with the members of your Facebook group. It's exactly like the game sounds. Post one picture at a time and ask your members to guess the location of the picture. This is an idea that real estate mogul and Shark Tank investor Barbara Corcoran uses. She posts a picture and if a member guesses the correct place, she gives away a signed copy of her book.

The Before/After Tactic

Independent Pools has done a great job so far with my Green Lion soup pool. They're spiffing it right up!

Here is a before and after of a house I sold. It was an investor/flipper who picked it up. I had a local pool company come out and get it cleaned up. I posted a bunch of before and after photos, and the pool company made a good split shot of the before and after. I took that, put it on my page, and gave him a thumbs up. I also got him in front of a local builder who I am partnered with. Again, it's about building relationships. Plus, people love a good before and after shot- why do you think HGTV is so popular?

Event Invitations

If you're hosting an 'Event', invite your members to it. But remember to be practical about it. Avoid inviting the people who live on the other coast to a local event. Also, when you're hosting your kid's birthday party, be sensible and invite only your friends and family. Invite members to events that are not so personal.

Feature Other Agents' Listings

You may also consider asking another agent in your office if you can market their listing. I have personally done this and let all of my agents market any listings I have. The ad however needs to be written correctly and should include great pictures. Noah Mandel spoke about Facebook ads and I've put my spin on the subject and given screenshots of some very successful Facebook campaigns that I've run on my page.

A Picture-Perfect
Facebook Post

Adding Value to Your Page

Whenever you sell a home, request the buyer's permission to click a picture of them standing in front of their brand new home, keys in their hands, smiles on their faces and, if they have one, a pet nearby (you know Facebook users LOVE a good pet picture). After you get the perfect shot, post it on Facebook. Here is an example of a caption you can use for your business: "Green Lion Realty would like to welcome Mr. and Mrs. Henry Smith and their dog Fido to their new home in Punta Gorda Isles"

To give the snapshot and caption some more weight, post some more pictures of the beautiful water view that shapes the back drop of their home or any such beautiful sight that would enrich the sale value of that particular community. Finally, end it with something like this: "If you're looking for your dream home in PGI give Green Lion Realty a call."

You can also put up pictures of new home buyers on local Facebook pages as a way of welcoming your clients to the new locality.

Real Estate Videos
For Facebook

Facebook now has over 8 billion daily video views. If you aren't creating video content specifically for Facebook, you are really missing out on a big opportunity to get more leads.

It's easy to get started but you do need to know a few things in order to be effective. You can't just take any old video, stick it on Facebook and expect it to get views. Your videos have to be specifically optimized for Facebook.

So let's take a look at exactly how to do that!

Facebook Live Video

Facebook's live video streaming option is extremely popular. So popular, in fact, that people spend 3x longer watching live-streamed videos on Facebook than videos that are not live.

It's not hard to see why Facebook Live Video is so popular. It offers people the chance to engage with the video creators in real time. It's exciting and fresh and has a 'breaking news' vibe to it.

As well as people loving Facebook Live Video, people are also more likely to see a live video thanks to Facebook's algorithms. Facebook Live Videos are more likely to appear high up in a user's Facebook News Feed. The bottom line is that live streaming is extremely hot and you need to take advantage of it.

You're probably thinking, 'That's all well and good but how can a REALTORS® make use of Facebook Live Video?' Here's one idea that will really set you apart and help to establish your brand: use Facebook Live Video to stream a virtual open house.

We've already established that the power of the internet gives you access to potential buyers from all over the world. There are tons of interested prospective buyers who might not be able to make an open house in your area. But they would definitely watch an open house live and enjoy the ability to ask you questions in real time!

There is amazing potential right here and few of your competitors are doing it right now. Swoop in now, while it's still fresh, and you'll benefit greatly from being first to the party.

Keep Your Videos Short And Sweet

Facebook states that videos under 2 minutes hit the sweet spot. When you're not making live videos (which are going to be much longer), you should amass a collection of videos that are around the 2-minute mark.

Facebook users, and people in general, are busy, have short attention spans and are being constantly bombarded with distracting content. So have a clear point when making your videos and don't take up too much of their time.

But what should you do in those 2 minutes? There are lots of things you can do but your aim should be to make the viewer glad they chose to watch your video. You want to teach them something, entertain them or make them say, 'Wow!'

For a great example of impressive and shareable real estate video content, check out SouthFloridaLuxury.tv. They've got a ton of videos that are 2-4 minutes long that do an excellent job of showing off their luxury properties. Here are some of the techniques they've used to create beautiful video content:

Professional video clips of the properties spliced together to keep it interesting (e.g. 2-4 seconds per room).

Different camera techniques (e.g. panning shots, close ups, zoom-ins, zoom-outs, aerial shots).

Upbeat sound track:

It doesn't take much to get your videos looking as clean and professional as those. All you need to do is hire a licensed drone user to get some aerial shots of your listing, hire a professional to film the interior and then some basic editing skills with a free software like iMovie and some royalty-free music will round it all off.

'How-to' videos are also incredibly popular. Make a bunch of how-to videos based on questions that clients commonly ask you when selling their house or buying a property. You could do a whole bunch of home improvement tricks and tips. This will further position you as an authority. Show yourself as an expert that helps people and, when it comes time to buy or sell, people will approach you.

The Facebook Interest
Gaining Technique

Adding Value to Your Page

When you post things on Facebook, you need to heighten people's interest so that they can keep coming back to you in hopes of finding more interesting things. Try writing something like this:

"Holy cow, 9 days on the market and I already have an executed contract! Who do you know who's looking to sell in the Venice area? Contact me!"

Post a picture of the home to go along with the statement to add punch and impact. You can also write about the things you do during the day such as listing homes, selling homes and showing property, etc.

Another thing you can do is leveraging shared articles, like we talked about earlier. Here's how I managed some great engagement after sharing someone else's article on my page. It was titled, 'Why We Love Sarasota.' Above the article, I wrote a statement that read:

"The 1905 salad at The Columbia Restaurant is to die for! Definitely worth stopping in if you're out on St. Armand's Circle."

My decision to write the above statement totally paid off because someone posted a comment on my page below the article. Here is the actual comment:

"We had one last night- a meal in itself- shared a picture of their famous sangria- TO DIE FOR IS AN UNDER STATEMENT!!"

After reading this thrilling comment by a certain Paula, I replied to her post by making the following comment:

"That's great!! There's another Columbia Restaurant in down town Ybor City, which is also very good. Paula, you should also try Kilwin's, great ice cream."

Paula responded to my comment with an enthusiastic, "Already did both!" and I posted a follow-up comment and responded to her by saying:

"Wow! You're way ahead of me! Feel free to post any other cool things you're doing. I always love to see cool things that others are doing in town!"

Now, if you're wondering about the logic behind this, let me enlighten you. This post did a few good things. The article I originally posted was written by a friend and happened to be loaded with useful information for people living in or visiting the area. So, I not only gave away good quality information to all of the members of my Facebook page, I also connected with one of them via the comments mentioned above. Plus, the more comments on a post, the more likely it will show up in people's news feeds, expanding your reach exponentially!

Always remember one thing; if your page merely consists of some listings, you aren't giving your members what they came in search of: value! If the members of your page find that it contains nothing of value, you can't expect them to stick around for along time.

When I post a suggestion, recommending people to eat certain things, they realize that I've actually been to that particular restaurant and I'm giving them advice based on my personal experience. Also, the business I'm referring benefits from this since they are getting free advertisement from my high praise and, obviously, they are going to love me for doing so.

Now here is another significant thing that happened after I posted my opinion in this situation. Paula commented on my post, praising the business even more. When this happened, Google immediately saw that as a subject of high relevance and brought my page and the conversation with Paula to the fore fronts of search engine visibility.

The restaurant I mentioned has a large audience in the form of tourists who visit them. Each time anyone searches this restaurant on Google, I'm going to pop up on the search engine results for this restaurant. And naturally, if anyone happens to be in search of a home in my area, they will contact me and be in the running for my potential clients.

When people randomly search for the best restaurants in town, guess who will appear in the results? That's right, it's me! The friendliness reflected in the conversation I had with Paula scored me a few extra points for being a real estate agent with a polite, friendly and approachable nature.

Think Outside the Box with Your
Facebook Page Content

Making your Facebook page interesting will get you more visitors and clients. Most importantly, it will keep your page fans and followers always excited about what you will post next. So what exactly do you write about? Here is an idea you can use. It's yet another example of the kind of things you can post on your page to make it fresh and interesting.

The title of the piece could be: My New Friend, Adam. This is what I posted.

Meet Adam. He lives on the streets of down town Sarasota. I went to downtown at the recommendation of my good friend Paul Edward Anarumo. He recommended I grab a bite to eat at the Drunken Poet Café. Well, it was closed down for renovation, but sitting right in front of the Café was Adam. It was almost like he was placed there for me to see.

He asked me if I had any spare change and I asked him if he'd like to go grab a bite to eat. This made him a bit nervous and he was reluctant to leave his supplies there. In fact he was shocked and told me that he isn't presentable enough to enter the upscale restaurants of downtown Sarasota. I said, "Well, why don't we just grab a bite to eat out on the patio at Evie's Restaurant?" He then reluctantly agreed.

Adam told me he's from Woodstock, NY and he traveled here because the weather was getting too cold for him to be outside. He isn't working now because someone stole his wallet and he has no identification at the present moment. I Googled some information on how he could go about the process of getting a new ID and I wrote down the addresses and information on how he could do so.

My assistance seemed to bring within him a sense of obligation to help me out too and in exchange, he told me about a dog food named 'From' that he used to feed his dog before it passed away. He also told me about something called Nordic that's in the health food store and mentioned that it is good to give my pups.

We then talked about how hard it is for him to sleep out doors with all the swarming mosquitoes. He mentioned something called Herbal Armor that came in a green bottle that is great for keeping them away. He also had some really cool pink salt he used on his food.

I thoroughly enjoyed my afternoon with Adam and I think he enjoyed spending time with me too. I gave him a tuna fish sandwich to have for dinner or to give to a friend back at camp.

Stop and take some time out to simply listen to someone and help them out. It could be the new agent in your office or even the homeless guy who was confused about how to get back his ID.

Please meet my new friend Adam.

#SarasotaHomeless   #HelpingHandUp
#DowntownSarasota #Sarasota

If you want to find a way of getting clients, post your experiences. Be genuine, be helpful and do a good deed. That's what it is all about, building the interest of people by posting simple acts of kindness.

Another example of how I do this started off with an idea from my 11-year old daughter Iris. She took all of her Christmas money, roughly $100, and donated it to the local animal shelter. She then challenged me and every business in town to do the same. Her goal was to raise $3K in three months and she's almost there. For example, she asked her orthodontist to donate, our vet, Petland, the coffee shop and many other businesses.

Iris also wanted to hold a pet adoption event. So now, once a month, I sponsor a dog adoption event at my office. I take pictures weekly of all the dogs that need homes at the local shelter and keep up with them when they get adopted. People log on to my Facebook page to see who still needs a home and to read what I write about the dogs that have been adopted. I keep track of everyone who donates money at my dog adoption event and thank them on my Facebook page. I also get the media involved. My local paper writes an article every time we have an adoption event and they also include the names of the people who donated money and how much they gave. They also put pictures of the dogs, along with Iris trying to get them adopted. This is free press for my company and it's a great thing to do in the community, a win-win situation!

Chapter Checklist

Now you have everything you need to create fun, engaging content on Facebook that your users will love and share. Soon enough, you'll start to notice your efforts paying off with more and more leads contacting you for your real estate services! To recap, here's how to get started producing the best content through all of your Facebook channels:

- Create and share quality content from a variety of sources
- Source quickly and easily by following local pages
- Create the perfect post
- Gain interest and push the envelope with personalized content

Chapter 9: How to Manage Your
Facebook Pages for Longevity
Social Media Etiquette: Best Practices for Your Facebook Posts

Invest Time in Practicing Responsiveness

Social media is all about interacting with one another, sharing your thoughts and opinions and responding to people when posts, comments, suggestions or queries are addressed to you. Therefore, when people start responding to your posts, answer them, immediately if you can, and avoid procrastinating at all costs. If you say you'll reply later, you may forget to do so and lose a potential lead.

Not being responsive is also a sign of carelessness and an I don't care attitude, which is contradictory to their perception of you being a trust worthy real estate agent with a great amount of expertise under your belt. My motto is to respond to potential clients within 5 minutes. If you dont respond quickly then another real estate agent will. After all, if a potential client called your phone, you'd respond right away, wouldn't you? Adding things to your page, without the intention of ever responding to others, is never going to benefit you in any way.

Keep Spammers at Bay

The Internet and even social media platforms are filled with spammers and you should not allow them to post on your page. You can spot spammers among the people who join your page because they'll start trying to sell items like diet supplements, sunglasses, mascara, etc. Allowing these sort of things to be posted on your page is harmful because people will start viewing it as a page where basically anyone can post anything. This will not attract people to join in; in fact, it will do the exact opposite. When you find these posts on your page, delete them immediately and ban the person from becoming a member.

A Personal Real Estate Page Isn't the Same as

Your Personal Facebook Page

Create a personal real estate Facebook page that is not the same as your personal page on Facebook. For instance, Shannon Moore, SW Florida REALTORS®. When people are in search of a real estate agent on Facebook, they are most likely to search for something like "SW Florida REALTORS®". They will not be searching for your name unless they know who you are.

But by adding my name to SW Florida REALTORS®, when they search this particular term, my name and page automatically appears in the results section. It's easy and free advertising! Here is how you can create a personal real estate page for yourself on Facebook:

- Go to your News feed and on your left, where you should be able to see 'Pages'
- Click on the option of 'Create a Page'
- Then click on 'Local Business or Place'

A window should then pop up, telling you to 'Choose a Category' and obviously, as a REALTORS®, the category you would want to select for your page will be that of 'Real Estate'. Under this, there is a sign that reads, 'Business Place or Name'. This is where I put "Shannon Moore, SW Florida REALTORS®".

Remember, what I want is to capitalize on people looking for a REALTORS® in the area of SW Florida. It will then ask you for 'Street Address, City State and Zip Code'. This is where you put in your office information, NOT your personal address. Facebook will then ask you for your 'Phone Number' and you should add in the number you will most likely answer when your phone starts to ring. It's better to add in your cell phone number as opposed to your office number so that you're always on call for potential clients.

The next step is to click on the 'Get Started' button. When you click on it, you will see the first page, which is the 'About' page. It starts off with 'Category', where you type in 'Real Estate'. Once you're done with this, you will be prompted to pick a subcategory. I picked 'Real Estate Agent, Real Estate Investment and Real Estate Service'.

Directly below this box, you will see a sign telling you to add a few sentences to inform people what your page is all about. This part is important, as it will help you appear in the correct search results. Going to the option of 'Page Settings', you will be able to add in more details. Here, you can add in things, helping others to get acquainted with you by reading more about you. You can add in things answering questions like:

- How can you help your clients?
- Why do they want to use you as an agent? What is your experience?

My bio tells people that I was born and raised in SW FL. In this section, I also talk about the fact that I attended local schools, as did my kids. I mention this on my page because a great number of people are eager to know about the schools in the area. As a matter of fact, it is one of the top things people ask me.

I talk about my experience working with investors and the success I've had. I also talk about my recent sales and the fact that in my first year in real estate, I sold $10 million. This particular fact is quite note worthy and is a great way to let people know that I'm really good at my job. But I also want to connect with people on a personal level, so I talk about things I enjoy doing in my area such as going off to the beautiful beach, boating and kayaking.

I mention the things I enjoy doing because you want them to imagine doing such things too when they move into the area. Paint them a beautiful and enticing picture where they are sipping a refreshing margarita with their toes nestled within the soft and smooth sand. (Have I mentioned I love living in Florida?) Remember, you're not just selling them a home. You're selling them a lifestyle! My bio comes to an end with me talking fondly about my dogs because, as I've previously mentioned, people generally love animals.

Next is a box which you will need to have for your website. This is important because if you don't have one, people will start building a perception about you not being well established in the real estate business. This is why you need to link up your site here. This is how you can go about it:

You will be asked whether you are a real estate establishment, venue or business, to which you need to click 'Yes'. Then you'll be asked if you are the official and authorized representative of the establishment, venue or business on Facebook. The next thing you need to do is to click on 'Save Info' so that you can move on to the next section. This part is where you select your 'Profile Picture'. Facebook will present you with an option of either uploading a picture from your computer or importing one from your website. One thing to be sure of when uploading your picture is that it should be a recent one, so that people can recognize you easily if and when they approach you. For example, I like to change my hair color on a frequent basis and each time I do, I also change my profile picture. The reason I do this is because I want my picture to look exactly like the person who will be meeting them, without any surprises. There's nothing worse than a client staring at you in wide eyed amazement because of the huge difference in your appearance and your profile picture. Also, make sure the picture you upload is professional, high quality and one that is free of any background distractions. It's best to find a place with some nice foliage and natural lighting to set the backdrop for your picture. Also put someone to the task of shooting your picture- no selfies!

When it comes to picking the clothes for your perfect profile picture, wear something you might wear when you're out showing property to your clients. For all you lovely ladies out there, a nice suit or blouse is the way to go, while the men can go for a collared shirt, tie and jacket to showcase your professionalism in your picture.

Once you have the right photo, pick it out, upload it and click on the option of 'Save Photo'. When you are done with these steps, you will see another page called 'Add to Favorites' and, upon clicking the button with the same title, you will be able to access it easily at any given time. After this, click on 'Next'. You will then have to move onto the next step, 'Preferred Page Audience', where Facebook will ask you the people you'd most like to connect with. What happens is that basically anyone can find your page, but after you have given Facebook your preference, it will use this information to put your page in front of those who matter most to you.

This is also the place where you can narrow down your target audience on the basis of age, gender, location and interests. I generally leave this open to all since I believe my target audience is scattered all over the world. Click 'Save' after you've made your selection and voilà! You're done with your personal Facebook page for your real estate business.

The Nitty-Gritty of Managing
Your Personal Business Page

After you've successfully created your personal business page, here are a few pointers to help you better manage what you're doing:

There is a tab called 'Page' which you can find at the top left of your page. This tab includes every single thing you may require for managing your page. If you want to view the messages you've received from your potential client base, you will be able to find it in the 'Messages' tab.

Right next to the 'Messages' tab, you will see two more tabs. The 'Notifications' tab is where you can view all your notifications and the 'Posts' tab is where you will be able to locate all your scheduled posts. Remember, Facebook is all about interacting with one another. After you've created your page, encourage people to visit and 'Like' it.

A little tactic to encourage likes is to show some support for your effort in setting up your Facebook page by liking it yourself. This way, when people visit your page, they will know that someone else, even though it's just one other person, has seen your page. The right hand side of your page will allow you to keep track of the number of 'Page Likes', 'Messages' and 'Notifications' you have received for the week. Talk about incentive to keep up with your posts! Make it fun by competing with yourself to try and beat out your statistics from the previous week.

Your profile picture appears to the left of your page and, directly above it, you will be able to see the camera icon. Upon clicking this icon, you will see a message that says 'Add a Cover', after which you can click on 'Upload Picture'. This is the place where you upload your cover picture. The picture you upload as your cover should be interesting enough to entice people to move to your area.

Lastly, you need to click on the 'Reviews' tab and it will ask you to 'Tell People What You Think'. When you reach this option, click 5 stars and then start writing about ways of helping out your clients. Another thing you need to do is encourage all your clients to rate you on Facebook or any other social media platforms.

Outsource Your
Graphics & Content With Fiverr, Upwork & 99Designs

We've looked at a lot of tips for putting out online content in this book. While I'm sure a lot of it has made you excited and your eyes have lit up at all the possibilities for more business, I'm sure you're also feeling a little overwhelmed.

"How can I possibly get all of this done? How can I find the time to make tons of videos and share them across different platforms? How can I find the time to craft blog posts? How can I find the time to post on Facebook, Twitter, Instagram, and so on?"

Time is our most precious resource. As REALTORS®, we are acutely aware of that fact. There is never enough time in the day. We can try to make use of pockets of time throughout our day in order to post on social media. But that still might not be enough to spearhead an effective marketing strategy. Luckily, we have some options.

You need to properly outsource and delegate.

There are tons of different ways you can outsource some of your marketing but the three I want to focus on here are Fiverr.com, Upwork.com and 99designs.com.

Fiverr

Fiverr will be your 'bread and butter' site for all things graphics and design. As the name implies, this is a website where you can hire freelancers to do small tasks for only five bucks.

You will need to spend more than a Fiverr in order to find a freelancer you like. Go into the website prepared to do some investigating. Check out the samples provided and solicit a few different people in order to test-drive their work. It's best to try and find someone you can establish a long-term relationship with so that you can keep your branding consistent and you don't have to waste time searching for more freelancers.

Fiverr operates by presenting you a range of 'gigs' that you can purchase. You see what someone is offering, you send them a message as to your requirements and then you pay them $5 or more in order to commission the work.
Here are just some of the fantastic things you can get designed on Fiverr:

- Custom Facebook covers and banners
- YouTube banners and avatars
- Blog post images
- Business cards
- Infographics

99Designs

99 Designs is a website where you can get a website, logo, business card, car wrap design specially tailored to your liking. You submit a design idea or ideas and graphic designers from all over the world begin creating designs for you. If you do choose a design you will work with that designer until they get the design exactly correct. The page gives a full money back guarantee, so I you dont like any, you dont pay. Ive had great luck hiring designers from this site.

Upwork

Upwork is where you will go to get content and ghostwriters for your blogs and different platforms. You will want to spend more on this website. How much is totally up to you but the old saying rings true: you get what you pay for.

Go into this site searching for someone that can be your long-term 'go-to' writer. You might need to assemble a team of writers, so don't be afraid to interview and test out a few different people. You can always set a writer a task as a trial, pay them for their time and then make a decision to keep working with them based upon the quality of the content they produced.

Upwork is a very different compared to Fiverr. It's very much a buyer's marketplace and requires you to post a job detailing what you need. You will then get freelancers – often an overwhelming amount – applying to your job.

Hiring someone is a tedious process but here are some tips to make it slightly less painful:

Put a code word in your job listing. Explain that the interested freelancers must put this word at the very top of their proposal. This will help weed out generic cut-and-paste proposals. If you get proposals that do not use the word, you can assume they didn't read your post and you can discount them.

Discount people who are competing on price. When you post a job, you have to set a rough budget. If your budget for a job is $10,000, you don't want to waste time reading the proposals of workers who offer to do the job for $5.

Discount people who have a poor grasp of the English language. You're hiring content writers here. If you can't understand what they are saying to you in their proposal, discount them immediately.

Once you've got a stable of reliable writers and designers, you'll be well equipped to attack social media with relentless force. Time will no longer be an issue. I recommend you check everything that your people produce for you to make sure that it's on point and aligns with the image you want to present. I also recommend that you do your fair share of posting on social media so you can keep your finger on the public's pulse.

What You Need To Know About
Facebook Services

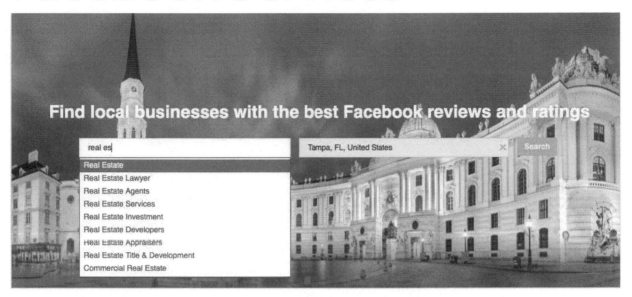

Once you've got a handle on all things Facebook, a great way to reach even more clients is to use the newly released Facebook Professional Services. It might be new but that doesn't make it difficult to use. If you've mastered everything else on Facebook and know how to use websites like Yelp, you'll be able to use Facebook Professional Services very easily. It's not too big just yet but I encourage you to get there early because it's definitely going to grow and grow.

Facebook Professional Services is basically a directory for local businesses inside Facebook. This helps people find businesses in their area with Facebook ratings and reviews.

People use keywords to search for local businesses or they can browse through the top business categories in their area. Once they have made a search, customers will see details about local businesses, like address, phone number and ratings. Having your business listed on Facebook Professional Services really is a no-brainer because it gives your visibility another boost. So let's take a look at how to get started with it!

Facebook Professional Services: First Steps

There are five steps you need to follow to get your business set up with Facebook Professional Services. Once you've followed these steps, we can play around with adding a services section to your Facebook page.

1. Choose the correct category and subcategories

This is incredibly important. Facebook relies on this information being accurate to ensure that your local business page appears in front of the right people. You need to search using keywords that your customers would use to find you. Luckily, Facebook provides a helpful dropdown menu of suggestions when you type something in.

Enter these keywords into the Page Info of your business page by clicking the "About" tab.

2. Fill in your business details

Next you must ensure that all of your business details are filled in. Fill in things like address, hours, short description, and phone number.

3. Enable check-ins and star ratings

When you edit your address, there will be a box beneath the map. The box says, "Show map, check-ins and star ratings on the Page". Check this box. It's important because you will build up social proof whenever someone uses your services and decides to let Facebook know. This will also allow you to add individual services on your page (which we will discuss in a second).

4. Create a call to action

When you're editing your page, you will see a button next to the "Like" and "Message" button that says, "Create Call to Action". Click that and you will be able to create a "Call Now" button for mobile users and sync your "Contact Us" with your website's contact page. This is important because it gives clients multiple ways of contacting you and makes contacting you much easier. You also want to add a 'Message' button so that clients can contact you through Facebook private message.

Once you've got the basics up, you should let your clients know that a review or a "check-in" would be greatly appreciated. Most people are hooked up to Facebook via mobile so it doesn't take much effort for them to check-in, leave a rating or quickly type out a review.

Now let's get into the fun stuff and add some different services to your local Facebook business page.

5. Adding Services To Your Page

Once you've got a local business Facebook page, you can start adding individual services in order to show clients exactly what you can do.

First, go to your Facebook business page and click the "Services" tab in between the "About" and the "Reviews" tabs. Then you want to click the blue "Add a Service" button. You'll be confronted with a box that allows you to name your service, set a price, write a description and add a photo. You'll want to make sure, as always, that you choose a compelling photograph to advertise your services. I recommend it be professionally shot, relevant and work well as a thumbnail.

Here are a few ideas for services you can offer:
- Investor/Builder Relations
- Marketing Expert
- Distressed Property Help
- For Sale By Owner Assistance
- Market Analysis Of Your Home

Get creative. What can you offer to your clients? What services have you provided recently that received good feedback?

Once you're finished adding services, click the "Published" slider on the left of the page. This will make your services visible to searching clients and visitors to your page will see your three recently added services above your posts. Visitors will see a snippet of information about each service and will have to click on it to see more, so make sure the first line of the description is enticing and relevant.

People can't purchase these services but, if they're interested, they can click the call to action button and get in contact with you to discuss further.

You may not wish to outright set a price and instead focus on getting your prospective clients on the phone first to discuss. If this is the case, I recommend you simply put your phone number in the "Price" section when you fill out the service information.

The key with Facebook Professional Services, like everything in this book, is to play around and experiment until you find something that works best for you.

Get Active with
Local Facebook Groups

Post on Online Yard Sales

When I initially started promoting my business online, I used to contact people by going to their online yard sale pages on Facebook and posting things like, 'If you'd like more exposure for your home, you're welcome to post it up on my page for free." Quite obviously, almost everyone jumped at this opportunity.

There are around 100 pages online related to yard sales in my area and the majority of them have anywhere from 2,000 to 30,000 members. I've liked all those pages that allow real estate posts; in fact, most of them do, if you don't overdo it. Make sure to always read the rules prior to posting. After I started posting things on these Facebook yard sale pages, word started to spread and people started informing their relatives and friends as well. Remember, everything you do online quickly has the ability to become viral.

I try posting something on all of the websites every week. Sometimes, I post about an open house, or a new listing, or perhaps a client who just reduced their price. This is free advertising to hundreds of thousands of people in your area. Now here's where I put a little spin to it. Each time I sell a home, I give my clients a paper with the addresses and links to the local online yard sale or community pages. I also add them to the page and introduce them and when this happens, everybody welcomes them. There are times when I have around 20-30 clients on one page and whenever anyone posts in search of real estate, they tag me and say something nice about me.

This is a tactic that works really well and it's free so you have nothing to lose. You should try it!

As a side note, some people say none of the online yard sale pages allow RE posts. Here's my answer: If you are unable to find any that will allow you to post, then your best option is to just be active on the local community pages and try to help people by answering their questions. I have people recommend me to others when they are looking for an agent just because I'm helpful to people on the page.

How To Have A Great Open House Turn Out
With Local Yard Sale Pages

I'm going to let you in on a great little tip for getting an excellent open house turn out by using Facebook Yard Sales. We've already touched upon this tactic but it is worth stressing it again here because it will really help boost your open house turn out.

The next time you have an open house, go to Facebook and search for local yard sale groups and pages in your listing's area. You're going to share your open house information in these places. Share the information on at least 50 local yard sale pages. You read that correctly. Let me say that again: at least 50 pages.

Some might say that's overkill but it's not. The more pages and groups you share with, the greater the turn out. If you just share the information with a handful of groups, you might not get any takers. The people in those groups might not see your information or they might not be interested or they might have other obligations. That's why you've got to cast a wide net.

Try to share your open house information in groups that have a high member count. An average group count of 15,000 members is a rough guideline to follow. Let's do some quick Math. If you share your open house information in 50 local yard sale groups and the average member count of each group is 15,000, you've just extended your reach to 750,000 local people for free. And some of those people are going to be very interested to check out your listing.

There are many reasons why posting on local yard sale pages is great exposure. Here are a few of them:

- People often obsessively check their Facebook groups multiple times a day. You have a high chance of being seen.
- When someone comments on something in the group, it goes up to the top of the group's feed. This means that if someone comments on your open house information, more people will see it.
- You can communicate with group members via private message. You're bound to get interested people popping up in your inbox.
- Group members are notified when you post something.
- People will often "tag" their friends in the comment section of your post if they think they'll be interested.

If you want to heap a little extra coal on the fire, I recommend you do a $200 Facebook ad two days prior to the open house. Set the ad to end on the day of the open house. This will give your efforts a real boost right when you need it. This will also ensure that you reach over a million people in your area for only $200.

Become a Member of Local Facebook Groups

Log in to Facebook and become a member of the local groups that generate a huge amount of traffic. In addition to yard sale sites, you can choose to join groups such as local restaurant reviews.

You can basically join any group as long as it fits the criteria of having a large audience and the probability of someone seeking the services of a REALTORS®. If people are posting their home FSBO, encourage them to post on your Real Estate News and Updates page.

Make them aware of the fact that it is free advertising and, after viewing your information in their news feed for a few months, there is a pretty good chance they will contact you if they're unsuccessful in selling their home. You can also start promoting your group on several other Facebook groups if the group rules allow you to do so.

Chapter Checklist

There's more to using Facebook for your business than just sharing posts daily. There are both practical tips for best use as well as official rules to abide by. Knowing both helps your page stay in front of your audience so you can continue engaging them on a regular basis. Always remember to:

- Use basic social media etiquette on all of your pages and groups
- Keep your business page separate from your personal profile
- Stay up to date on Facebook's official rules

Chapter 10 : Win-Win Relationships

How to Leverage Personal Connections

There's no denying that social media is a powerful marketing tool. But nothing can ever replace the power of face-to-face networking, especially for a real estate agent. The golden key to success? Combining your real life contacts with your social media strategy to create win-win situations for both you and local businesses and other partners. Here are some of my favorite tips for creating some amazing opportunities for cross-promotion.

Promote Local Businesses with Facebook Tags

Facebook tags are a quick and easy way to promote local businesses. Let's look at an example. Suppose you go and purchase some tiles at a local tile store in your town. Snap a few good pictures and post some of your best shots, displaying some of the most striking, unique and absolutely neat tiles, and tag the store in the post. Remember the Word Swag app I talked about earlier? This is a great way to use it.

Show the store owner or manager your post and ask if you can leave a stack of cards at the business for them to hand out. They are surely going to appreciate the fact that you not only purchased tiles from their store, but also promoted their business on your page. Because of this chance to attract more customers and seeing what you did for them, they'll likely be extremely glad to return the favor by handing out your business cards to their customers.

The Welcome Bag

This is really more of a win-win-win: it benefits you, your business contacts and your new contacts. Go around and visit a few local businesses and explain to them that you are assembling gift bags for all of your new residents whom you have recently sold homes to.

It's best to visit the stores you think will lend you a helping hand and whose owners are of a friendly nature as they will be easy to persuade into helping

you. When I went to local stores in my community, the local hair salon put in a trial size shampoo and conditioner and a note to go along with it, which read, 'Welcome to the community. 'Their advertising information was also printed on it.

The Crepe Café threw in a free crepe and drink coupon. The vet contributed a free pet exam and the local car wash added a free wash to the welcome bag. This is an excellent way of making my clients feel welcomed and connected with the community they have joined. And since the welcome bag is not something everyone just hands around to their clients, it will be a first for them and they will greatly appreciate this gesture from you.

What else will the welcome bag do for you? It will give you referrals from all of the businesses in town that have helped to assemble your welcome bag. I can tell you this works as I've done it myself. In fact, the local businesses love the fact that they get good business from me several times a month. This is why whenever anyone is on the lookout to either buy or sell, they are happy to recommend me to them. Now imagine this: you're putting up a welcome bag for your clients and, in return, almost every business in town will be recommending you to their connections! Take this relationship online by recommending these businesses on your Facebook page. You need to start living by the rule of working smarter, not harder.

The Coffee Giveaway Tactic

Here is another thing I've done that has worked for me in a small town. While you are enjoying a nice hot cup of coffee at a local cafe, buy coffee for the next 15 to 20 people who walk in. Ask the establishment to inform those people that the coffee was paid for by you.

I've used this tactic quite a few times and I've had people come up to me and thank me for the coffee. Oh, and that's not all. Want to take a wild guess about what other benefit I got out of doing this? That's right, I have received leads more than once from this coffee giveaway tactic.

Once people come to your table to thank you, you can strike up a conversation and, if they or anyone they know are looking to buy or sell in the area, you can refer your business to them. Considering your act of kindness, they may approach you for your real estate services too. And, of course, always make a Facebook post about where you are and maybe mention someone you met while at the café.

Pop-Bys

You can deepen personal relationships and encourage referrals with both current and past clients by sending out a "popby." If you're not familiar, it's a small gift that reminds them of your service. Here is a great example from one of my Facebook group members, Mary Harmon Young. She was inspired by the website Popby Ideas (http://www.popbyideas.com/) which is full of ideas for all kinds of seasonal popbys. Browse the site for new ideas every month. But first, check out Mary's results after leaving these postcards and sparklers on her clients' doorsteps over the Fourth of July holiday

Business Exchange

This is another idea that came to me when I was having a meal at a nice local restaurant on the waterfront, where I was greeted by the sight of a fishing boat captain walking into the restaurant with some fish.

I asked him if he was open to the idea of me taking a picture of his catch so that I could post it up on my Facebook page on real estate news. I was extremely happy to hear that he loved my idea and I posted some exciting pictures of him along with his clients posing with the fish.

The caption I put up with the picture read something like this, "If you're in search of an excellent charter captain who can haul in the fish, give Captain Smith a call at 941-222-2222." I was also sure to tag his Facebook business page in that post for people to obtain more information.

In return, I handed him a stack of my business cards and asked him to be kind enough to pass them on to his boating clients. This simple idea is a win/win solution for both sides because he will promote my business to his clients and I will promote his business to my clients. And all of this is basically free advertising!

I also offered to promote him further whenever he has a charter and asked him to send over some pictures and to let me know whenever he needs more of my business cards. On the back of your business card, have discounts for local mom and pop businesses-restaurants, carpet cleaners, car washes and then refer businesses back and forth with them.

Two examples of businesses referring me to clients in 24 hours include a carpet cleaner and an insurance agent.

Traditionally in real estate, people tend to talk a lot about your SOI. They generally tell you to call your Aunt Betty and let her know you're now an agent, then call your cousin in Colorado, who you probably haven't spoken to in 20 years, and let them know too.

But I like to include people who are going to be talking to potential clients on a daily basis. This is why I approached people like the Stanley Steemer guy, the lady in the café down the street, the guy who gives kayak tours to tourists, my dentist and so on.

But a word of caution when promoting businesses: I only approach a business after I've given them something and after I know their reputation. I don't just work with any business in town. I do my research because I want my clients to have a good experience with them. If they don't, I'll be the one to get blamed, taking a blow to my own business. This is why you can't just approach any business.

If I've referred them, their business becomes a reflection of me and my business too. Now let me tell you what I mean by the words, "I've given them something." It means that I've shared their products with my page and have either endorsed them or sent them some clients.

As a general rule, I never ask for something unless I've given them something first. This is why door knocking and cold calling don't work for me. So, after you've tagged them in a few of your posts or sent a few clients their way, your next step is to approach them to form a business relationship. If you can get approximately 30-50 businesses in town sending you business opportunities, it can be a huge push, especially for a new agent. So do put in your best efforts in trying to accomplish this.

The Alternative to Knocking on Doors

Are you tired of knocking on doors? As you can tell, I never like it. If you don't either, use the alternative. It's a much better idea anyway. In addition to partnering with brick and mortar stores, try having your friends and business partners, those that go in to people's homes daily, recommend you to their clients.

If you're wondering who people will call when they are getting ready to have their home sold, let me tell you who their go-to person is. They call one of my good friends, who also happens to be my business associate, and he goes by the name Jeff Klinebriel from Stanley Steemer.

Here is what the conversation will be like:

Jeff: Hello Mr. Seller, I'm here to make your floors shine.
Mr.Seller: We are getting our home ready to put on the market.
Jeff: Oh, that's fantastic! Do you have a REALTORS® to help you out?
Mr.Seller: No, we don't. Do you happen to know a good one?
Jeff: As a matter of fact, I do. Here's her card.

Mr.Seller: That's great, thank you so much. I'll call her right now!

Jeff Klinebriel also happens to be a preferred vendor in my 'welcome bag'. Just as he recommends me to his customers, I return the favor by gladly referring him to all of my clients. Think about the amount of homes he steps into on a daily basis, and many of them will be possible clients who are looking to sell their homes.

After doing his bit by recommending me to his customers, he tags me on Facebook to give me a heads up that I'll be getting a call. Jeff is such a good friend that he even stops to place my open house signs back up when the wind blows them away.

You also need to find a few trustworthy references in the form of home inspectors, title companies and other contractors who can refer clients back and forth with you. This will give you another source to acquire new clients based on third party references as to your credibility and worth.

Let all of your friends and business associates learn the scripts so they can land you some new clients, but do remember to return the favor by recommending them to your clients as well. This way they will have your back knowing that you have theirs.

Bulletin Boards and Business Cards

Always keep a few essentials in your car: a stack of your business cards, some clear business card holders and a secure baggie with push pins. Whenever you make a new business partnership, you'll be prepared to leave your cards behind if they have counter space or a bulletin board for you to take advantage of.

It's easy to incorporate this into your online strategy. I have a page set up on my website that I use to recommend various local businesses. If any one of my clients uses the services of any of the businesses I've recommended, I always ask them to mention my name.

Let me give you a better understanding of how this works with an example. When I go out to eat at a restaurant where the food is just fabulous, I ask to meet with either the manager or owner upon finishing my meal. I then compliment the delicious meal I've eaten and tell them the things I liked about it.

After complimenting them, I ask them if they have a Facebook page, a website and other pages like Yelp or TripAdvisor. All of the people I've used this tactic on loved the idea. Below the link, I may post a comment on the things I've had at the restaurant. Then I post this onto my website and on Yelp and TripAdvisor or any other social pages they have.

I also ask them if it is fine with them if I leave some of my cards to distribute to their customers. Remember, it's best to give something before you ask for something in return. Everybody should win!

The Rank Request

Start requesting satisfied clients to rank your service on all social media platforms such as Facebook, Trulia, Zillow and Rankmyagent. You can ask them to do so by sending them a link. The reason why this is important is because people like reading reviews to get an idea of whether people are enjoying your service or not. People regard online reviews very highly these days and when they are unaware of who you are and don't have references from local friends, online reviews and service rankings help them to find out more about you.

My For-Sale-By-Owner

Listing Tip
Create a Website for FSBO Listings

So how exactly do you get an FSBO to list with you nearly every single time? This tip generally works 95% of the time (at least it has for me). Here's something I did about five years ago and let me tell you something, it worked really, really well. In fact, I'm actually sad I didn't keep up with the page. I didn't stick to it because I got into remodeling homes and let some other things slip too, but I'm going to explain to you how it worked out for me and why it still works.

I remember getting a company named Real Pro Systems to make the page. You can probably make it yourself if you're the tech savvy type or you can also choose to hire someone from a site like Fiverr to make it for you.

Here's what you'll need to do. You first need to create a simple one-page website and it should be equipped with a place where clients can upload three or four pictures and add around four lines of text.

When clients go to the page, they are able to:

- Upload a few pictures (not enough to properly showcase everything they want to in their home)
- And add a few lines of type (not enough to say everything they want to about their house)

But here is the thing: it's a free place to list their house! Now this is where it gets interesting. When I implemented this tactic for my own business, I used to send them a letter that would read something like the following:

WILL ADVERTISE YOUR HOME FOR FREE AND YOU WILL NOT OWE ME A COMMISSION IF YOU SELL IT!!!

I would then go onto explain the ways through which they can put their home on my page for free. I used the letter to explain how it will go out in my signature line of every email I send out and all of my other marketing efforts. This website would be one of those efforts. Who wouldn't be jumping up and down because of free advertising? 95% of the people definitely will!

I started out having it just for my little town and soon hundreds of people were on my page. If I remember correctly, I called it ByOwnerNorthPort.com. Gradually, people from other states started asking me if it was OK to post their homes on my page as well. Because of this, I now recommend avoiding using a specific town in your URL. When I made mine, I didn't really think it through completely, nor did I expect it to go so well. Using a specific town alienates all other towns and states, therefore it's best to use a URL that's more generic.

Initially, I was hesitant about the idea. But then I thought to myself, why not? I could simply refer them out if it wasn't a listing for my town. A great number of people sold their homes from the page and they spread the word and told so many people about what I was doing. It was crazy and amazing at the same time. As time went by, it turned into a pretty huge deal.

Here's another thing I did. People had to give me their phone numbers and email addresses to post, in case people wanted to buy their home. I took their email addresses and placed them into an automated email campaign and personally wrote more than 60 emails that went out once every week.

I would say something like this:

"If you plant bright flowers in the front of your home, it might sell faster."

Then I'd have a picture of a home with bright and beautiful flowers out front and explain the importance of pictures when it comes to selling a home. After all, the first thing people lay their eyes on is the front of a home. I got a huge response to this because it was a personalized tip that was actually very effective and didn't at all resemble anything like spam.

I'd also ask them to send me a before and after shot so I could see how it looks. I would receive a ton of email responses saying, 'Here are my before and after shots, what do you think?' Some of them would also ask for my opinion and recommendations for making the images more appealing.

After a few more emails based on my advice and recommendations, they would invite me to come over and have a look at their house and to have it listed. I would always keep a record of all the emails I sent out to them and used that to point out the things they did and didn't do based on my recommendations.

When I went out there to list, I would say something like this:

"I see you did really well with planting the flowers in front but WE need to work on getting the kitchen counters de-cluttered, like I recommended in the email I sent to you in July. WE can do this! You're almost there."

As you can see in the above statement, I would emphasize the word 'WE'. People love to be recognized for their accomplishments and become eager to show you the alterations and changes they've made. In the event of them not using any of my suggestions, I would usually say something like:

"WE can work together on this and we'll make a few small changes to get your house ready to list."

When you give people personalized tips that actually help them a great deal, they start trusting you and appreciating your advice. It's just like what we talked about with social media: being sincere. This is why FSBO sellers used to call me when their efforts at selling their homes themselves didn't pay off after around six months. They called me because I was the nice agent who was kind enough to help them out by providing them with free, highly effective tips and website listings.

Basically, you're acting as no more than a newspaper ad for that FSBO. As a real estate agent, the only thing you really need to consider if you opt for this method is that you should give a written notification to that particular FSBO and let them know that you're acting in a 'NON-REPRESENTATION' format. When you do so, it will allow you to obtain buyer results from that page in an ethical manner. Also remember to make buyers register for more details.

My FSBO idea worked extremely well for me but it took up a whole lot of my time. I would personally answer each of the phone calls and emails and would take some time to go and visit their homes.

This was when I was handling a huge amount of house remodels per month, which is why I couldn't spare the great deal of time that goes into all this and so I didn't continue with this tactic. But if you're just starting out, or are in a slump, this is a great method to boost your listings.

Alternatively, you can also target FSBO listings on Zillow and reach out to them offering the same information and tips based on their post. It takes less time than building a website and has the same targeted reach.

Securing Builders

Here is another tactic I adopted that you can use for your real estate business, no matter where you are in your career. In fact, just this month, I picked up two new builders. The first one approached me to take care of their marketing after noticing the fact that I had advertised a great deal on Facebook.

See how social media marketing pays off? I found the second builder myself and admired their floor plans, so I asked them if they would hand me the opportunity to market their product for them.

If you were to view my page, you would see a Facebook post I had made for them. I went on to post it on over 80 local yard sale pages, each of the pages holding the strength of about 2,000 to 50,000 people. So it is basically free advertising for them! I then boosted the post to reach an even wider audience.

This led to another opportunity when the first builder that asked me to market his homes wanted to know my thoughts on layouts, amenities, and price. I hadn't been in the new build game for years and I told him I needed to do some more research to be able to give him an honest opinion.

I took one of my newer agents and went around to 30 different local builders. I wanted to see their product, look at their prices and ask questions. I also pulled up permits for the two counties I was interested in targeting. I looked at what was selling, how long the permits were taking, what sized homes were the most popular, and who was buying most of the homes.

I noticed that many of the competing investors were now flipping new builds. I took this piece of information back to my builder to discuss with him and make his product stronger. A few things we had to be careful about was not to over-improve, compare comps and make sure to price them correctly so they would appraise well if the buyers were getting a mortgage.

While I was out looking at builders, I fortunately ran into one who had piqued my interest due to quality and price. We had lunch together, talked about his product and the tactics I use to market homes. Because he had a ton of other real estate agents approach him to market his product, he wasn't too interested in my pitch.

However, we worked out a deal that he would let me market one of his homes off the MLS. The only thing I could use was social media and, not meaning to brag, I brought him 71 hot buyers in less than two weeks! That impressed him quite a bit and they now want me to market the entire area they service. This is an example of how a strong online audience can really let you be nimble and respond well as new opportunities crop up.

I have one builder who caters to the more affordable side of housing and one who caters to the mid- to high-end clients. Before I made any agreement with the second builder, I checked with my first builder to make sure he didn't have any issues with the relationship. So when you're dealing with builders, be open, be honest, be helpful, and be truly interested in your clients and seeing them do well. You will start noticing that it works out really well.

Another approach I use is to solicit vacant lots and then ask the lot owner if they would have any objection to me marketing their lot with the builder's home on it since this will most likely lead to a quicker sale. You shouldn't be surprised to discover that this idea is loved both by the builder as well as the vacant lot owner. Before you do this, make sure that you check with your MLS to ensure this is OK. My MLS just recently altered the rules and they say that you must have an agreement between the seller of the lot and the builder.

Another way to target new builders and vacant lots is by running a specific Facebook campaign. Here's an example of a previous ad I've run:

"Looking for lots in Englewood FL. Do you own a lot in Englewood FL or the surrounding area? I have a unique marketing plan to sell your lot. Call The Moore Team for more info! Shannon Moore, Green Lion Realty, 941-276-8142 or greenlionrealty@gmail.com."

In addition to the ad text, I also include a pretty picture of a sunset to grab people's attention. Once I have the lot listings and have talked to the owners about listing the lot with a proposed model then I reach out to a new builder. First I talk to the builder about listing their homes on one of the lots I've secured. Even if the builder has hundreds of floor plans available, it's best to select just one to pair with the vacant lot listings. Vary the model type so that the MLS isn't oversaturated with the same pre-construction pictures.

Your next step is to get the owner of the lot to agree to let the builder market their home on the lot. This isn't too difficult because the builder typically pays the commission on the lot sale, which is very appealing to the lot owner. The reason they do this is because the listing is free advertising for the builder. Lots of people contact me about the home listed in the MLS. Even if the prospective buyer doesn't want the specific home or lot advertised, they still might purchase something else from the builder. It might be a different floor plan and a different location, but the sale could still come through. It's the same concepts as an open house. Buyers usually don't purchase the home they come to view, but you could still get their business through another listing.

Chapter 11: How to Go Viral on YouTube
(Without Being an Expert Video Editor)

The YouTube Blaster

Everyone is aware of YouTube and millions of people post videos on it. You can use this great website to your advantage with my YouTube blaster idea to give your real estate business a helpful push.

This is what the YouTube blaster is all about. Go out and visit the local community, taking pictures along the way. When you go by the club house, the pool, or the tennis courts, click some beautiful pictures. Try to make the shots as interesting, vibrant and appealing as possible.

When you return, use a free movie editing program such as iMovie to convert the pictures into an attractive slide show. This program and several others are easy to use and best of all, FREE!

Add some nice background music to the slideshow directly from the program and add in your contact information at the beginning and end of the movie. You can add information including your name, your designation, the name of your business, your website and your phone number. Also remember to give your movie a catchy title before you go ahead and upload it on YouTube.

When people Google your community, your YouTube video will appear among the top pages, giving you free advertising forever. This not only helps you attract more business, you also get to learn a few things about your community in the process.

One pro tip I can give you is to try and keep your videos under two minutes. People tend to get bored easily and at times, even if the topic is interesting, they tune out and start viewing something else if a video is too lengthy.

Community-Specific YouTube Videos

Another great way to add content to your YouTube channel is by making videos for separate communities. I currently have around 189 videos for the various communities where I reside. Remember to create each video with exact specifications of the community; for example, Heron Creek North Port Real Estate. By creating these community specific videos, interested buyers can easily view the perks of living there.

People wanting to sell their home in those neighborhoods will also get a chance to see what a great job you do listing your clients' properties.

At a later stage, I purchased an entire library of professionally shot photographs for a total of $2,000 from a local photographer. So make an effort and visit the community yourself and, while you're exploring the places there, try to capture some great shots of things like the pool, the clubhouse, the community center and the workout rooms. Then bring home your pictures and turn them into video slides with free software like iMovie.

I would suggest you include something like the city or state or the community name to your movie title. It will be helpful for SEO and general searching purposes. Google owns YouTube and you will notice that videos often pop up at the top of search engine results. It's kind of like having your business card at the very top of every community in town, free of cost.

The Video Creation Idea

I don't just happen to be in real estate. It seems as though I received a calling. In fact, it seems like a legacy as far as my family is concerned. Most of my family is in the real estate business- my mom, my middle daughter and even my youngest.

My middle daughter was lucky enough to make it onto The Ellen Show at the tender age of 14. She confidently talked about real estate on the show and her impressive manner earned her many more interviews nationally as well as internationally (185 interviews to be exact).

My youngest one, who is 11, came up with a brilliant idea for how to create real estate videos. Her fabulous idea helped me out a great deal and in the last three months I've scored several sales, all thanks to her. She makes all kinds of videos and it's been a great way to involve her in my business. I know many parents wonder how you can sell real estate and have kids. Get them involved! My daughter does videos about selling homes or about investing and I post them on my page. My clients absolutely love them!

Here are a few examples:

How to get good deals at Lowes
11-year-old house flipper evaluates home
Top 10 types of people who live in FL
11-year-old house flipper. "If I can do it, so can you!"
The four main components of a house

Chapter 12: Utilizing National Media Outlets
On Local News Stories
News jacking to Reach Millions

Each time new stories relevant to my area pop up on national news sites, I start posting on threads like NBC and CBS. For instance, I live in SW Florida, and I'm pretty sure everyone was aware of the terrifyingly huge alligator on the golf course that received the privilege of being featured on the front page of just about every major news outlet in the country?

Well, when I read the story, I went to each and every website and Facebook page that posted the golf course alligator story. I then posted, "Hey, if you'd like to snuggle up to a big gator, give me a call, I sell real estate in SWFL". I included my website and contact information below my comment and guess what? By the end of the day, I had over 300 emails that mentioned how funny the post was because the one thing people absolutely love (besides cute animals) is humor. My funny post landed me about 30 to 40 great buyer leads.

This literally is free advertising! All you require is the perfect timing so that you know exactly when and where you need to post. People are always busy with their lives but two things everyone makes time for are humor and animals.

News jack on Your YouTube Channel

A while back, US News posted an article about Punta Gorda, a local town I service. This story became a front-runner by getting splashed and quoted all over the news not only locally but nationally and internationally as well.

When this happens in your area, here is what you do to create a relevant YouTube video that automatically tops search engines when anyone searches for the article.

133

- Grab an exciting story as soon as it becomes a national headline
- Create a headline for your YouTube video that's very close to the headline of the news article that has gone viral.
- Add in a few attractive slide show pictures of the area.
- Throw in some statistics and let your audience know the value of the great town.

Be sure to include your contact information, then simply sit back and watch the leads roll in. I have made it a habit to keep a close watch on my Facebook news feed for breaking news stories. Your video should have:

- Positivity and optimism
- The capability of going viral
- The capability of being quickly relatable

Take Advantage of Click Bait

Newspapers are always writing articles I refer to as 'click bait.' I use this particular term because they are constantly encouraging you to click the link to view reports, lists, and so on. They write and publish such stories about every single town in every single state.

Let me give you an example to help you understand this better. Recently there was an article in USA Today that read, "Top 10 Beaches in the US." Thousands of people all over the world clicked to view the contents of the article. One of the beaches mentioned in the top 10 list was Siesta Key Beach, which happens to be in my selling area.

Now, if I'm one of the first people to comment on that article, about 500,000 people will see my comment when they read the article. I may post a comment that says something like this:

"Siesta Key Beach has sand made out of quartz and is fine as baby powder. I love living in Paradise!"
Shannon Moore, Broker/Owner, Green Lion Realty, 941-276-8142
greenlionrealty@gmail.com, HYPERLINK "http://www.greenlionrealty.com/"

500,000 people will then have just seen my contact details without me having to pay even a single dime for advertising my business online. Think out of the box to start noticing your customer pool getting wider with each unique tactic you adopt.

Print Media Advertising Tactics

I've mostly talked about online marketing, but there's still something to be said for good old fashioned newspapers. Another way to grow your brand is to start writing about the areas in your community and have them submitted to local newspapers or media outlets. Newspapers, a form of print media advertising, are always looking for opportunities to fill in the space. If they get a well-written article including a few good pictures, they eat it up like candy!

To grab the attention of newspapers, you can write an article about the real estate market and its current situation, including well researched statistics to support the content presented in your article. You can also choose to write about a particular community you specialize in.

For example, when you write about a community, mention note worthy statistics, like its sales shooting up by 10% in the past three months. You can also mention the average number of days on the market, the number of homes that have been sold recently in the development, accompanied by their average selling prices.

After having submitted a certain number of articles to newspapers, you will start to receive calls from them inquiring about new stories. From their point of view, if you possess knowledge about several communities in the area, you are most likely going to have information about general real estate.

Since I have adopted this tactic myself, there are two local newspapers that on average call me once a week. They conduct interviews with me to get my opinion about things like:

- The foreclosure rates going down
- The changes taking place in the local flood zones
- The current market situation

They also ask me things about the local economy. Now here is some food for thought. If my name and company gets mentioned in the papers every single week for free, what are the chances of potential clients calling and contacting me? Well, my chances are extremely good!

People are most likely to call the person who has been quoted in the paper week after week due to my expertise and knowledge of the area I represent. I started out small and then worked up to several articles in The New York Times, NPR and other media outlets. Be the authority in your area and you will be the first priority for the people who are looking to buy houses in your hometown. And of course, any time you're featured in a publication, share the online version (or a photo of the print version) on your social media outlets so that your current audience gets to see you featured in these news outlets.

Willow's Story:

How My 14-Year Old Daughter Purchased a Home

Part-1

I've had a lot of people PM me and ask what the story is about my daughter. Willow was enrolled at a local full time gifted school. She has an extremely high IQ in addition to ADHD - kind of like keeping 20 cats in a box. Willow was at this school from 2nd through 7th grades. She began to really struggle in middle school and the guidance counselor convinced me to put her on medicine to help her concentrate. Willow turned into a zombie, lost her appetite and had to drop out of soccer because her weight plummeted so low. She still wasn't keeping up in school. She had no motivation. I was homeschooling her little sister and I gave her the choice to drop out and have me home school her. She agreed. The day we took her off the medicine she began to blossom again.

I told her that she was going to have to go with me when I work with my flippers. She hated the idea at first. Then she began to ask me questions.

"Why did you pick that tile? What counters make sense for this house and why?" Then we went to a home my flipper had just purchased and it was filled with stuff. She asked me what the flipper was going to do with it all. I told her she could call and ask him. He told her he had to get it all out of the house ASAP. She asked him if she could sell the stuff and split it with him. He said to just sell it and keep the money.

Part-2

Willow then began to scour the neighborhood on her skate board on trash day and get things people put at the curb and sold them. She would also get things like Jordan shoes, football and basketball jerseys, electronics and skateboards from Goodwill and sell them to people on Facebook or her friends. She saved $6k in a short amount of time doing this.

Fast-forward three months. We're at the dinner table and I'm talking to my husband about this great home I found in Port Charlotte that was only $16k. Willow is listening to all this and says, "Do you think they'd take $12k?" I said, "I don't really know, why do you care?" She said she wanted to partner up with me. My husband was totally against the idea. He wanted her to get a paper route. She said she'd come up with a plan and tell us her idea the next day.

I thought it was a great idea! I could teach her how to measure for tile, how to interview contractors, how to interview tenants, how to turn the water and electric on at a house, and other things. My husband hated the idea. Willow's idea was to split the cost of the house and then take her half of the rent money to then pay for her half of the renovations. With her selling business and the rent money she bought me out of the entire house within six months. She had just turned 14.

She Rolled That Money Into Flipping Two More Homes

Remember how I told you I get interviewed a few times a month by the local paper? Well, my good friend Michael Braga with the Sarasota Herald called me and said a reporter called him from NPR and wanted to get a few quotes from a local broker who would be straight up about the local real estate market. "No 'it's a great time to buy' BS," he said. He gave her my name and she called me for an interview. It started like any other interview. We talked about my investors and she said, "Can you give me an idea of how low the market is?" I answered, "If a 14-year-old can buy half of a house, it's pretty low." Then I started talking again about my flippers. She wanted to talk more about the 14-year-old girl. She said she's flying down from NY and wants to spend the day with Willow. We already had the day planned before she called and she just tagged along. She went to an auction with us, to Goodwill to pick up product and watched Willow make a $100 profit that day. She was with us from 8a.m. until after 10 p.m. After the interview, the reporter told us that the AP was going to pick up the story and that it was going to be big. I thought she was being nice and thanked her and she left.

Part-3

A few weeks later, the reporter called me and said the story would be going live that Friday. I was shopping in another town and almost forgot about it. Willow was with me and we jumped in the car a minute before it went live on NPR. We listened to it and thought it was kind of cool but didn't think much about it after that. Then my phone rang at 6:30 that night. It was a call from LA. I almost didn't answer because I thought it was Realtor.com or Zillow or one of those companies trying to sell me something. I did answer though.

The person on the other end of the phone said, "Is this Shannon?" I said, "Yes". Then they said, "Is this Shannon Moore?" I said, "Yes". They asked if my daughter was named Willow and again I said yes. The lady asked me if I knew someone named Ellen. I was kind of embarrassed that I couldn't come up with any clients named Ellen who I had worked with and certainly not from LA. I sheepishly answered no. Then the person said, "Oh, so you don't know an Ellen Degeneres?" I was like WTF? Really? Somebody is messing with me. It was her executive producer Glory Gale. She said Ellen heard Willow's NPR interview and loved her. She wanted to know if Willow was available to talk to her and if we could fly to LA the next day.

I went in Willow's room and mouthed that The Ellen Show was on the phone. Willow crinkled her nose in disbelief. Glory asked Willow if she wanted to come out and be on the show. Willow's eyes got really big and she said yes. Glory told her that her only stipulation was that she could not give any interviews to anyone else before appearing on the show. Willow said nobody cares about this story anyway. Glory replied that they do and they will be calling. Well, there were no calls on Saturday. Monday morning at around 2 a.m. I got a call from some Middle Eastern TV station and I asked them to call back at 8 a.m. By 7 am we had calls from Anderson Cooper, Good Morning America, The Today Show, Inside Edition, Fox News, CBS News, ABC News and hundreds of radio and TV stations both nationally and internationally.

Willow went on The Ellen Show on St. Patrick's Day and went on to do over 185 interviews. She did public speaking engagements with Miss Kay of Duck Dynasty, talking to business owners and disadvantaged children. She does regular round table discussions on investing and entrepreneurship with The Huffington Post. She was completely self-sufficient at 14, paying her own cell, clothes, groceries and everything else.

A month before she turned 18, she moved to downtown Chicago with her girl friend. She makes very good money every month (more than I do in some months) and is finishing her senior year of high school. I taught Willow a lot of the skills she uses when selling. She's a marketing whiz, way better than even me. She tells people, "If I can do it, so can you!" Listen to Willow and find something you're good at and capitalize on it.

Here are just a few links about Willow. Her name is Willow Tufano. If you'd like to read more you can Google her name.

Part-4

Here are some links for your reference:

The Ellen Show:
https://www.youtube.com/watch?v=GTTczC27fko

Teenage Landlord TV show trailer:
https://www.youtube.com/watch?v=7fDX5bhZuVc

CBS Evening News:
http://www.cbsnews.com/news/florida-teen-landlord-turns-foreclosure-crisis-into-opportunity/

NPR:
http://www.npr.org/sections/money/2012/03/09/148218539/this-14-year-old-girl-just-bought-a-house-in-florida

NPR second interview:
http://www.npr.org/sections/money/2012/10/12/162796828/remember-the-14-year-old-who-bought-a-house-she-just-bought-another-one

The Next Big Thing Radio:
http://nextbigthingradio.net/podcast/conversations-ep-15-willow-tufano

James Madison Institute and ABC News:
https://www.youtube.com/watch?v=4bt5_BQo8x4

CNN:
https://www.youtube.com/watch?v=w69gHqOvOhg

SNN News:
https://www.youtube.com/watch?v=Qp4LJ2KNW_M

ABC News:
http://abcnews.go.com/blogs/business/2012/03/florida-14-year-old-buys-distressed-home/

http://abcnews.go.com/Business/florida-teen-willow-tufano-buys-home/story?id=17490510

NBC Nightly News:
http://www.nbcnews.com/video/nbc-news-channel/49463491#49463491

USA Today:
http://usatoday30.usatoday.com/news/opinion/forum/story/2012-08-13/thrify-ben-franklin-frugal/57039184/1

Wharton University:
http://kwhs.wharton.upenn.edu/2012/12/lady-gaga-fan-and-landlord-willow-tufanos-real-estate-investments/

Inside Edition:
http://www.insideedition.com/headlines/4078-meet-americas-youngest-landlord

Fox Business:
http://video.foxbusiness.com/v/1525152573001/14-year-old-buys-foreclosed-home-for-12k/#sp=show-clips

Huffington Post:
http://www.huffingtonpost.com/2012/10/12/willow-tufano-buys-second-home_n_1962221.html

Learn Vest:
https://www.learnvest.com/2012/04/meet-willow-tufano-the-14-year-old-who-bought-a-house/

Daily Mail:
http://www.dailymail.co.uk/news/article-2217325/Watch-Donald-Trump-At-15-years-old-Americas-youngest-landlord-buys-second-home.html

I Times, Most Successful Young Entrepreneurs:
http://ww.itimes.com/blog/most-successful-young-entrepreneurs-willow-tufano

Jezebel:
http://jezebel.com/tag/willow-tufano

The Mary Sue:
http://www.themarysue.com/14-year-old-girl-buys-house

Chapter 13: Create Lasting Connections with Your Clients

Using the Power of Google

Building a sincere connection with a buyer allows them to trust you, which can in turn lead to a sale. If you really want to connect with your buyers before you even meet them, Google them! I have been in the real estate business for years now and I Google every single one of my clients before I take them out.

It makes for a great way of establishing a connection with them. Here is an example of how I use Google to help me out. Sally Smith was coming to town. I knew her name and the fact that her husband's name is Ron. She had also told me she works for Bill Gates and that she lives in Dallas, Texas. But this information was not enough to help me build a connection with either Sally or Ron. When I get to know my clients better, I gain a better idea of their tastes, likes and dislikes, aiding me to pitch my sale in the manner that will make them more inclined to accept my offer.

So I went on Google and typed in her and her husband's name, something like "Sally Smith Dallas Texas Bill Gates." Among other things, an article came up about a race she ran. Fortunately, my husband is a runner, too! So I spent the evening researching the best places to run in the area and also talked to my husband and asked him a bunch of questions on running.

The next day, I went to pick Sally up. I started a conversation and asked her the kind of things she enjoyed doing, all the while knowing that she enjoyed running. In accordance with my expectations, she told me she was an avid runner and she ran marathons. Thanks to Google, I was already aware of this piece of information and had therefore come prepared.

I talked about how my husband is also a runner and started chatting about the best places in the area to run. A successful sale is all about connecting with your client, coming prepared and being able to talk about their interests. I discovered a topic I could connect with Sally on and started building a connection with her.

This makes clients feel more comfortable and friendly around you and they tend to open up to you more. It's also great for your safety. You probably don't want to be driving around dangerous people and using Google, so you can also make sure your clients are safe people to drive around with.

Using Google AdWords

Google offers AdWords to help reach targeted search queries matching keywords you pick. Your ad can appear as a sponsored link at the top of the search results page or on websites visited by potential leads. Choose a few keywords, such as "real estate agent + your hometown" or "houses for sale + your hometown." From there, you essentially bid on your ad appearing in someone's browser. The price depends on how competitive your keyword market share is. If there are already a lot of people bidding for that keyword, then you'll have to go higher. The good thing is that your maximum bid isn't necessarily the bid you pay - you might get it for lower.

Additionally, your bid is for the cost-per-click, or CPC. That means you only pay when someone actually clicks on your ad link. This can be an extremely targeted, cost-effective tool to reaching people who are searching for to either buy or sell a home in your area.

Another good way of connecting with your clients is on the topic of pets. I have an agent who owns a Yorkie and I had a few more clients coming in who owned the same breed. I was able to obtain this information from their Facebook page.

Upon inquiring whether they owned any pets, they pulled out their iPhones and started talking fondly about their beloved Yorkies. Another amazing thing was that the agent I had brought along has Yorkies too and they started chatting and sharing their pup pictures and the pair soon became the best of friends.

Always remember to do your research before taking your clients out so you can be well aware of their likes and interests. Then you'll also know which direction to lead the conversation so that you easily converse about the topics that get them excited and put them in a good mood.

Utilize Google Alerts

Another idea you can adopt in your real estate business is using Google Alerts. Go to the Google Alerts page and fill in your name in the search, then save it. You should do this because each time you get mentioned online, you will receive an email with a link to the review or article you've been mentioned in.

This tactic is a great help in keeping you on top of your reputation while notifying you of a particular article you may have been featured in. You can maintain a record of all of the articles that feature you to add to your credibility. You can also make use of Google Alerts to find good content that has the potential to be shared.

Chapter 14: More Marketing Idea
How To Create A
Single Property Website

A single property website, as the name suggests, is a website entirely dedicated to one listing. You might think an individualized website just for one listing is too difficult and expensive but it's actually cheaper and easier to set up than you think. Single property websites, when done correctly, are also incredibly effective tools for converting interested prospects into dedicated buyers. This is because a single property website allows one to see everything about the listing all in one place. There are no other listings to scroll through and distract the viewer with. Ultimate importance is placed on one and only one listing. This makes the listing feel special and can result in your prospects quickly becoming very enamored with the property.

Top Characteristics of Single Property Websites

These are the elements that good single property websites often exhibit:

- One property
- Map and directions
- Lead generation form
- Property photo gallery
- Listing agent information
- Virtual tour of the property (e.g. with videos)
- Unique domain name. This is often propertyname.com

A good single property website must look beautiful. That means minimalist and professional design, stunning and professionally shot photographs, high quality virtual video tours, open house calendar and well-written copy.

In addition to making the single property website look fantastic, you should sync it to the relevant social media and online real estate outlets. You want your single property website to appear on Trulia, Zillow and Realtor.com and you want the video tours up on YouTube and Vimeo. You should also engage your Twitter, Facebook and WordPress audience. You will also want to ensure that the copy on the single property website has relevant keywords so people will naturally find your listing through search engines like Google.

Make Your First Single Property Website

You're probably thinking that you couldn't possibly make a website for every single listing. It would take a lot of time, effort and skills that you might not possess. Luckily, you don't have to register a ton of different domains or set anything up yourself. There are specialized companies that will do this all for you. They will set everything up for you and make sure that your single property website is aesthetically pleasing and converting. You just need to supply the details. It's worth shopping around to see which one of these companies is the best for your unique needs. They all have different prices, strengths and weaknesses. Some will charge you $50 per single property website, whereas others will charge $80. Some are better on design and functionality, whereas others are better on marketing. I recommend you check out listingsunlimited.com and homefinder.com/single-property-website/.

Even More
Marketing Strategies

Have you executed on the strategies and tips already outlined in this book? Have you established your brand on Facebook and YouTube? Do you and your writers blog, post and update on a regular basis? Are you consistently providing beautiful and shareable content that adds value to people's lives? Have you tried all of the paid and free marketing strategies? If the answer is yes and you want even more tips to boost your visibility, then read on for a few more simple-to-implement marketing strategies.

Start an Email Newsletter with Mailchimp

If you already have an established Facebook presence, you might wonder why you should bother starting your own email list. Well it's actually very important for a number of reasons. Ever heard the phrase, 'the money is in the list'? It's true. These days, building your own list is a golden strategy for success in practically any field. That's because people on your list have typically "opted-in" to join your newsletter. You put a sign-up form on your website and the people who like your content will give you their name and email. This is lead collection at its finest. You are not at the mercy of Facebook or YouTube or Twitter. You control your list and you have the power to use it to build strong relationships with the people on it.

But what do you do when people are actually on your list? Well, for one, you don't spam them. People guard their inboxes avidly these days. If they give you their email address, it's like they have given you a key to their house. If you spam them with constant sales letters, they will unsubscribe and you would have ruined a relationship. Instead, treat your email list in the same manner as we have described throughout this book. You are going to follow the 80/20-rule of giving mostly value. You want to build trust with your email list. You want them to look forward to receiving your newsletters. Here are a few ways you can do that:

Limit the amount of times you send email newsletters. Once per week is a safe bet. It's not too often to be annoying and not too rare that people forget they're on your list.

Send emails at the right times. Generally speaking, Saturday and Sunday is the dead time. Few people open their emails on these days. And if they don't open your email, how can you give them value? Good days are typically Thursday and Monday. The best time of day to get people opening your email is in the morning, around 7am. The best time to get people buying stuff from your email is in the evening.

Treat your emails like a conversation with a valued friend. Encourage your email list to share the email with friends or on social media. You should also encourage interaction and feedback. Tell them how they can contact you and ask them questions to get them involved. When people get involved, they will feel a stronger bond with you. And when it comes time to buy or sell a property, they will choose to use the REALTORS® they have a strong bond with.

To get started with your email newsletter, I suggest you use mailchimp.com. This service is free for your first 2,000 sign-ups but there are pricing options if you want to get fancy. The support is great and the emails are very intuitive. Once you've signed up, you will be able to get a sign-up form code that you can paste straight into your blog and then you can start collecting leads and building relationships.

Discover Hot Trends with Buzzsumo

If you need ideas for blog posts, buzzsumo.com should be your first port of call. It will really help you figure out what's trending so you can write relevant content that gets shared and commented on. Type in keywords relating to your niche, for example 'real estate Florida', and Buzzsumo will offer you all manner of related articles from across the web. They will also tell you how many shares the content received on Facebook, LinkedIn, Twitter, Pinterest and Google+. This really helps you cut out wasted time blogging on subjects that people will not be interested in. With Buzzsumo, you already know what people want to read so you will know exactly what to write.

You can also be one of the first to comment on these popular articles. This is good because, seeing as many of these articles go viral, you will be seen by a lot of people. For example, if there is a popular article about the best beaches and it names Siesta Key as one of them, I could write a blog post about how Siesta Key has powder white sand that is made of 98% pure quartz. Then I would comment on the viral article about the beaches and put a link back to my beach article. This is a great strategy because you're not spamming anyone. You're offering more valuable content that is relevant to what people reading the article are already interested in.

Guest Blog Posts

After you've racked up a good number of your own blog posts and you have spent some time consistently commenting on articles, posting in forums and adding value on social media, you should be in a good position to write guest posts on other blogs. If you have done things correctly and not spammed people, you will have built yourself up as an industry authority. You will also have made lots of connections and got to know who the big players are in your online niche. It is now time to use some of the authority and goodwill you have built as leverage in order to appear on other blogs.

Why would you want to write on other blogs when you have your own platforms? There are many reasons but the main reason is that you will benefit from even greater reach and social proof. Other bloggers have their own circles and their following of people might have never heard of you. But if you post on their site and offer true value, your circle will immediately expand to include many of the people in the other blogger's circle. Get in contact with people already in your circles and offer to provide something of value to their audience.

If no particular blogger or website comes to mind, you can always use this tactic to find places where you can guest post. Simply type the following into Google:

- Your niche keyword + submit a guest post
- Your niche keyword + accepting guest posts
- Your niche keyword + guest post guidelines
- Your niche keyword + post written by
- Your niche keyword + writers needed
- Your niche keyword + write for us

Explore, Experiment, Engage

This tip is perhaps the most substantial one I will offer you. And yet it doesn't involve giving you concrete instructions. I'm not about to tell you exactly what website to go to or exactly what technique to use next. Instead, I'm going to offer you a piece of advice that is very easy to overlook when you've read through a book as practical as this. If you've read through and applied everything in this book, you would have gained a very competent grasp of some of the most effective social media and marketing strategies for your real estate business. But much of the specific advice contained in this book may not be relevant a few years down the line. The basic premises underlining the strategies will remain the same but the platforms will evolve and adapt. We're talking about Facebook today but what platform will we be talking about tomorrow?

The most effective thing you can do is to explore for yourself. Don't just follow advice blindly and expect it to always work. You must consistently keep up to date on the latest technological changes and make sure you are experimenting. We're in a very exciting time in history right now and technological innovation is moving faster than ever before. Don't get left behind. If your child is playing around with a new app, check it out yourself. Ask them what it does and figure out if it's something your audience will soon use. Read the technology section of the newspaper and keep up to date with the latest start-ups. Constantly ask yourself whether you can get any mileage out of these new innovations. You will do well as long as you keep your eyes open to the possibilities around you.

The Story of Your Name

What's in a name, you ask? The name of my company is Green Lion Realty and I am often questioned, "Why that name?" As you can probably tell, I'm a person who is very interested in marketing. So let me break down the concept for you:

Green- I chose the color green because it gives off a good feeling - money, green building, luck, etc.

Lion- I know I've probably mentioned this one too many times in the book, but people really love animals. Think about the Geico Gecko, the Trix bunny, Tony the Tiger and many other very successful advertising campaigns. I wanted the name of my company to be something strong and bold. There's my lion.

The Logo- My logo is a lion's head door knocker. The reason I chose this as my logo is because it ties in with real estate, especially luxury real estate.

An interesting fact is that in alchemists times, Green Lion meant gold. The first name I actually thought of was Green Door, but I ended up opting for Green Lion instead. I'll just say make sure you Google any name before you go with it.

Next let's take the example of my book, Out of the Box Owl:

I wanted to convey that the ideas in my book are "out of the box" because most of my marketing ideas are original; if not, I put a different spin on them to maximize my success. I also wanted an animal that symbolized teaching and learning—what better animal than an owl, right? I believe my good friend and agent Nancy Ryan Schulman came up with this, if I remember correctly. I also required a tag line and another agent of mine, Chandler South, came up with the original tag line and, to make it a little tongue and cheek, we put a spin on it and called it, "Not your basic pitch marketing!"

So there you have it. That was my story. Now that you have all the tools in your belt to create a truly robust online marketing campaign, what will your story be? I can't wait to find out.

Chapter 15:

How I Do a CMA

How to win a listing nearly every time. Be prepared, confident and honest.

As many of you may know, I recently hired on a new REALTORS®. She reminds me a lot of my daughters and I've taken a special interest in making sure she succeeds. She started at another brokerage and has only been licensed a few months.

Today I got a request for a CMA. I text her and asked her if she was familiar with how to do one. She texts back that she is. Then I got to thinking, does she really, really know how to do one? They probably haven't trained her like I want my agents trained. So here goes.

When I get a request for a CMA there is a lot of research that I do before even starting on the home evaluation.

First, I pull up the property on the local property appraisers site. This will tell me many things- what they paid for it, any improvements done to the home and who the builder is. I am very familiar with most of the local builders so I start to form a picture in my head of the layout and potential features of the home. Obviously, looking at what they paid for it will give me a glimpse of what they might be looking to sell it for.

Next I go to online permitting. This will tell me if there were any permits pulled on the home for electrical, roofing, A/C, hot water heater and things like that. So, if I go to the listing appointment and they tell me they had their roof replaced but I didn't find a permit for it, there might be an issue. I generally say something like, "I know your roof was replaced in 2004, the water heater in 2006 and the A/C in 2009, are there any other upgrades or improvements that you can tell me about?" Then they know you've done your homework.

Next, I go to the clerk of the circuit court website. I look for recent divorce filings, marriage filings, judgments or liens on the home, second mortgages and various other documents. This will give me an idea of their motivation to sell and the financial standing of the home.

Then I go to mugshots dot com or a similar page. I always go with my agents on listings appointments if they don't know the client. You can never be too careful.

I Google their name to figure out their approximate age and I look for news articles, Facebook, Instagram, Twitter and other information on them. This will prepare me for my conversation when we meet. I will study their profiles and know how I can connect with them. For instance, on a recent listing appointment the person was a runner. I knew this by viewing their social media accounts. The evening before I asked my husband about some of the local running trails around that aren't well known (he's a runner). During the listing appointment I noticed a framed running metal on the wall. I inquired about it and we had a long discussion about the trails, running shoes, running watches and other things related. I was prepared to talk about it.

I also Google the address of the home to find old Zillow and Realtor.com info.

After I have gathered my information I go to the MLS. I search active, pending and sold for the last 9000 days. I want to see if they're currently listed with an agent. If their house has ever been listed, for how long, with who and try to figure out why it might not have sold. I study the description, the price, the pictures, days on market and I look up any agent who has listed the property to figure out how they market their homes.

Then I begin my evaluation. I usually start with a half mile radius, no longer then 3 months back in solds, 100 square feet on either side and five years on either side of year built. Of course, I look at lot sizes, pools, extra garages and the like. Then I tighten or loosen my criteria from there.

Above all, be honest. I had someone come to me a few days ago who wants to build. When we met he said building really depended on what he got for his home. He thought it was probably worth somewhere are $500k. I did my evaluation the evening before and came up with a maximum price of $370k, on a good day. I was straight up with him on how I arrived at that price. I said that others might tell him he'd get more, only to reduce it drastically down the road. I simply don't work that way. It would have a very hard time appraising out at anything higher. I told him at this point, it doesn't make sense to sell his home and build. He was very, very impressed with my knowledge and honesty. I think they might still sell and build with me.

That's kind of a basic run down on how I prepare and what happens when I attend one. I rarely, if ever, don't get the listing.

Chapter 16:
Visiting Businesses

Hi Owls!

I've spoken several times about the importance of getting out and connecting with the local community. One of my agents was itching to find out how to do this and wanted me to show her how. We got on our walking shoes and hit the pavement around 10am.

I took the reins and we started out. We hit several restaurants, a custom glasses shop, a tile store and pet store and many others.

I explained that we wanted to get out and meet businesses in the community that we could refer our clients to. There was no charge and we would be featuring them on our Facebook pages and our blogs. All but one business were very receptive and loved the idea. The owner of one place we stopped in spoke to us about listing his $650k condo in the area.

She is going to set up a Facebook group called "The Review Chicks" and we're going to go out regularly review businesses.

Folks, get out there and make connections. Brokers, stop sitting behind the desk and get out there and help your agents be successful.

Chapter 17:

Road Map to Success

Many ask "how do you become successful." Here's how, step by step. Your road map to success.

My 9 step road map to dominating a neighborhood and real estate. You are going to be identifying 5 communities. First, type your city in to MLS and sort by subdivision. Then click sold for the last 3 months. Next figure look at the communities with the most sold listings. Are they areas that are a reasonable distance from your home or work? Many you want to focus on luxury homes or first time home buyers.

Figure out what's selling and who you want to be. Look to see what agent has sold the most homes in that neighborhood in the last year. What are they doing? Where are they advertising? Google their name. Also, Google the name of the subdivision and figure out what comes up on the first page. Most likely it will be Zillow, Realtor dot com, VRBO, Homes and so forth. You need to be on the first page of Google. We'll talk about that later.

Make a Facebook group. Make sure it's a group and not a page so people can be social and chat in it. You want to make it a closed group so it can be searched but people have to join the group in order to see what's going on. It makes it more exclusive and kind of forces them to have to join to see what's going on. Call it something like "Lakeside Plantation Friends and Neighbors" or you could just call it "Lakeside Plantation." If there is a sign for the subdivision, take a picture of that so when they look for the page, it's easily identifiable. Start posting things in the neighborhood- the sandhill cranes crossing the road, an announcement for the potluck dinner on Fri, the bocci ball classes, the great breakfast joint down the road. Then go and talk with the activities director and/or someone who is prominent in the community. Ask them to join your page and post events, happenings and whatever. Now you're ready to invite others to your page. Look at the rules on local yard sale pages and see if there is anything about posting your group to their group. Try to find groups with a lot of members. Usually because your group is not competition, it will be OK. Post something like- "Please come check out my group Lakeside Plantation exclusively (people like things that are exclusive) for residents of the community. We chat and share ideas about Lakeside. Your next step is to look up everyone's address who lives in the community and mail out a letter inviting them to the "exclusive" group. Nearly all will join because they don't want to be left out. Post mostly community stuff. Twice a month you can post a market snapshot of the community- average selling price, average list price, average DOM for the last three or six months. If something sells or is listed, you can mention that. If a home sells you can mail out a letter to the new resident welcoming them to the neighborhood and the group. Now you are the authority in the neighborhood.

Go walk the community and ask people what they love and don't love about the community, if there is an agent sitting a model, take a tour with them. They should know the details and possibly more than you know. They sell it every day.

This is your community, you need to know the amenities, the HOA dues, if they accepts pets, what kind, how large and how many, how close is it to the beach, anything unique about the community, about the builder, etc. If there are HOA dues, a map, membership requirements. You need to have a copy of them and be able to shoot them out to clients quickly.

Make a Facebook ad, you'll have to make it on your business page and promote it. Drop a pin on the specific neighborhood and only market to that neighborhood with your group.

Your next step is to make a Google AdWords Campaign. Watch this video if you're not familiar with how set up a campaign.

https://www.youtube.com/watch?v=zhSnj3jR_6c

After you watch that one watch this shorter video that is specific to RE: https://www.youtube.com/watch?v=PMqdiHKYNJo

Think of your 5 communities that you want to be the expert in. When we think of a a headline, we might use Lakeside Plantation Homes for Sale. The next line will be the benefit to the customer. Free list of homes in Lakeside Plantation! Then you can do a search on your website for homes in Lakeside Plantation and use that link in the destination URL. Like this:

http://greenlionrealty.idxbroker.com/idx/results/listings?idxID=b003&pt=1&ccz=city&city%5B%5D=33487&a_legalSubdivisionName%5B%5D=Lakeside+Plantation+04+Rep&a_legalSubdivisionName%5B%5D=Lakeside+Plantation+2nd+Replat&a_legalSubdivisionName%5B%5D=Lakeside+Plantation+Rep+01&a_legalSubdivisionName%5B%5D=Lakeside+Plantation+Rep+02&a_legalSubdivisionName%5B%5D=Lakeside+Plantation+Rep+03&a_legalSubdivisionName%5B%5D=Lakeside+Plantation

That won't show up in the search. You could use greenlionrealty.com or whatever your website is.

Under keywords I might put in:

Lakeside Plantation North Port FL
North Port Florida Real Estate
North Port Florida Realtor
Lakeside Plantation Homes for Sale
Lakeside Plantation Listings
Lakeside Plantation Realtor
Lakeside Plantation FL

Under the keywords you might want to exclude some keywords-

You can put a minus sign in front of the ad like this

-Lakeside Plantation Rentals
-Lakeside Plantation Lease

Create a shared negative keyword list
- Sign in to your manager account.
- Click the Accounts tab.
- Click Shared library from the menu on the left and select Negative keyword lists.
- Click + List.
- Enter a name for your list and add your negative keywords.
- Click Save.

Edit a shared negative keyword list from your manager account
- Sign in to your manager account.
- Click the Accounts tab.
- Click Shared library from the menu on the left and select Negative keyword lists.
- Select the list you'd like to edit.

To add negative keywords to the list:
- Click + Add.
- Enter the negative keywords you'd like to add and click Save.
- To edit existing negative keywords:
- Check the box next to the negative keywords you'd like to edit.
- Click Edit.
- Update the negative keywords you'd like to change and click Save.

To remove negative keywords, click Remove.
- Apply a shared negative keyword list to a managed account's campaigns
- Sign in to your manager account.
- Click the Accounts tab.
- Click the managed account where you want to add the negative keyword lists.

154

- Click Shared library in the menu on the left.
- Click Negative keyword lists.
- Check the box next to the negative keyword list you'd like to add to multiple campaigns.
- Click Apply to campaigns.
- Select which campaigns you'd like to add the negative keyword list to.
- Click Save.

Related links
Navigate and organize your manager account
Create and manage campaigns from your manager account

Or you can type the word in and hit the exclude button. Don't worry, you can't really mess up. You can remove, exclude or add things with the click of a button. You don't want calls or to spend your money on things you don't calls on.

Let's say you wanted to promote the new listing that I sent you over today, The Rio. You might make a title that says- New Construction On The Water $355K!

Your "hook" or the next line might be FREE DOCK and POOL. Then you might say, click here to learn more!" Then they would go to a landing page or a list of homes in that area. You'd have a description, pictures of the home and contact form. That ad would probably be very effective.

In the video, when he talks about ad extensions, do not click location. You need to click "extend my ad with a phone number" and type your phone number in. You want clients to call you and have immediate access to you.

As many of you know you can set up a new campaign in minutes. Wouldn't it be really neat to go into a listing appointment and be #1 on Google? Well you can! Right before the appointment you can set up an AdWords campaign targeting the neighborhood where the listing is located. For example, let's say the subdivision is called Lakeside Plantation. You might make the headline Looking to Buy in Lakeside Plantation? or maybe Lakeside Plantation Homes for Sale and target similar key words.

The question always get asked in listing appointments, where do people find listings and homes these days? The Internet, right? Ok Mr. & Mrs. Seller, let's do a search for your neighborhood. Boom! You come up at the top of the search results for that neighborhood when the sellers searches it. That's pretty powerful. Didn't we just agree that most people start looking for homes on the Internet? Wouldn't you like your home to be on my page about the community you live in, Lakeside Plantation? Absolutely! Where do I sign?

Here's another tip, There's a website called www.keywordspy.com I'm kind of in love with it.

Here's what you do. Type in a keyword phrase in Google that you think a client might type in to get to your page, like the example shown. Then you take those top websites and go to keywordspy. You can view ads your competitors are making, how much they are spending, what their ads look like, what their keywords are and who your competitors are (a side note here City-Data is out ranking most huge sites Trulia, Realtor and Homes). You need to look up the post I did on this page about City Data

Once you've done that, make or go on your Instagram account. Take interesting pictures of the community and begin hashtagging.
#LakesidePlantation
#LakesidePlantationRealtor
#LakesidePlantationHomesForSale
#LakesidePlantationRealEstate
#LakesidePlantationHomes

Go on your Twitter account (or make one). Tweet the community out- Lakeside Plantation homes under $200k!

Lakeside Plantation FREE summer kitchen with signed contract before May 1 (people love free stuff and it creates urgency).

YouTube videos. Go the community and shoot some pics and upload them into the Ripl app. You can make short little videos with that app. Alternatively you can just do a short video. Make sure it's not over 2 minutes long. People lose interest quickly. If you can add verbiage or subtitles, that's better.

Make a Blogger account and take about the community. Post your pictures, post what's going on. Make sure to mention Lakeside Plantation a few times in the article without being obnoxious. This will give you better SEO and help your blog to be indexed under your keywords. Don't just talk about communities. Talk about everyday stuff as well so potential clients feel as if they can relate to you.

City-Data.com is one of the best and most powerful places for free leads. Write a different blog about the community on their website. Google penalizes for duplicate content. Get on there and start begin social. Make sure to read my post about CD on the Owl page as they are very strict about advertising. Google loves this page because of the constant posts and interaction and you can rank a post within hours at the top of the search engines by using this page, and it's Free.

As you can see, I'm all about free marketing. Here's a tip I'm going to throw out and it has to do with getting your name in the local newspaper for free and having it in there at least once a month, if not more.

You start out by writing an article about a local community. Try to pick one that has some interest or one that would be interesting to write about. If I was looking for one to target one I might pick one that has pretty, historical homes, because they photograph well. I might also pick one that is selling like hot cakes.

So, now what you do is you go take pictures of the community. If you're not that great at taking pics then hire a photographer to take some pics. Find interesting homes or angles to photograph. Now write something about the community. People love historical facts. I will include a few snippets at the end of this post to give an idea of what to write.

Now what you need to do is include some statistical data, which can easily be garnered from your local MLS. I might say something like this: In the Towels Court neighborhood there has been a 52% decrease in the amount of foreclosures in the last three months. The average sales price is $576,000 and it's taking around 56 days for homes to sell. There are currently 23 homes for sale in this neighborhood right now with an average list price of $623,000. If you're not a writer then go to Upwork.com or Fiverr.com and hire a writer cheap to put something together. If you have the "meat" of the article, you can get someone to put it together for you.

The next step is to contact your local paper and talk to the real estate editor. Tell them that you've put together some great photographs and you've written an article about a local community and you'd like to send it to them for submission into the paper. Both of my parents majored in journalism, they've owned newspapers for years and I'm very familiar with the business and how it works. Let me tell you, if they can get a great prewritten article with excellent pictures--They are all over it. Oh and by the way. Stick your contact info at the end of the article.

So, now what you have is free advertising in the local paper (not many people read print anymore but all papers are now online). Your article is now posted online and when people search the community that you write about, your name will come up under those communities. If you've been quoted in the paper talking about this community, you must be the local expert, right? Oh and BTW, the ad that that fancy firm paid for that appears right next to your article is barely even looked at because your info is much more valuable than just a few listings on a page.

You need to do this twice a month. Here's what happens next. The newspapers will start to call you when they are writing about real estate because, after all, you're the local expert, right? Another thing, don't give the reporters a bunch of BS. They call me because they know they're going to get the straight scoop. I'm not going to flower things up and give them "it's a great time to buy" spin on everything.

Here are a few papers and articles I've been in and below this is some snippets of articles. I'm not going to bore you with posting all of the (because there are hundreds). I'll just post a few:

The New York Times:
http://www.nytimes.com/2011/04/08/business/08housing.html?_r=0

Herald Tribune:
http://www.heraldtribune.com/article/20150811/ARTICLE/150819937

Herald Tribune:
http://extra.heraldtribune.com/2015/08/29/ht-investigation-flippers-find-a-way/

Herald Tribune:
http://www.heraldtribune.com/article/20140424/ARTICLE/304249992

Charlotte Sun:
http://www.pgpcnprealtors.com/wp-content/uploads/2012/10/North-Port-Teen-Still-in-Demand_10.01.2012.pdf

Charlotte Sun:
http://floridasinnovationcoast.com/files/documents/9-11-15.pdf

Huffington Post:
http://www.huffingtonpost.com/2012/03/12/14-year-old-willow-tufano-buys-florida-home_n_1340452.html

A few snippets. Just Googled these and it looks like the paper has used these to spin into other articles in recent days, which doesn't help me but I love my reporters, so it's fine. Lol

Towles Court-Like Burns Court, The Towles area has some great, funky places. Towles court is home to many of our local artists: towles court artist colony Towles court was home to Mr. Gillespie's third home and his "Golf Hall". He named one of his courses The Links and today the main street running through the Towles area still bears the name Links Ave. In the 1920's Mr. Towles came to town and turned this section into an area for the business people and seasonal tourists. In the mid 30's and 40's this area was home to many migrant workers. And in the early 1980's Mr Olivieri had a vision of turning the area into a quaint little downtown neighborhood. In 1995, the first artist came to Towles court and now there are over 200 artist, shops, galleries, funky cafés, etc in the Towles Court area. Many are now paint bright, vibrant colors.

McClellan Park is one of my favorite areas and it dates back to 1916 when it was founded by two sisters. It is one of the oldest neighborhoods in Sarasota. The story goes that the McClellan sisters hired architects to divide "the park". McClellan Pkwy now runs through the middle of this area. During the early 1920's the sisters planted many palm trees, oak and other tropical plants. Many of these plants and trees still remain. There have been many archaeological finds in the McClellan area and it's thought to be an area of Native American significance. Many of the streets in this area are named for Indians-Mietaw Dr, Sioux Dr, Seminole Dr, etc. One of Sarasota's first schools McClellan Park school was built here.

I remember my grandmother talking to me about many of the areas I mentioned and I suppose that might be where some of my great love of the historical homes of Sarasota comes from.

You have now learned how to be the master on all types of media that matter. Go out and rock it!

Testimonials

The Podcast with Mary Shannon Moore

"This was a great podcast. I laughed, I cried and I gathered some great info. Thank you Mary Shannon Moore and Michael Oden! Also thanks for sharing your knowledge and making us all better agents!!"

- Jeanne Kay Pauls

Real Estate - Out of the Box Owls Facebook Group

"Hi Owls!!! Wanted to share my boosted ad results I did 7 days ago. Paid $40 and received 70 comments and over 12,000 reached. I secured 2 buyers (appointment on Saturday). I will be following up with over 20 leads who are ready to buy as well. My point is that if you're not boosting your ads, you're missing out on potential leads! Shout out to Mary Shannon Moore for all the help!!!! I LOVE this group!"

- Melanie Novales DePiro

Out of the Box Owl Book

"Just finished reading it- cover to cover. It is wonderful. Well-written, easy to read, informative and inspirationally motivating. This comes at a perfect time for me and I thank you!"

-Cynthia Sleppy Dodge

"Wow! I just started reading the book it's a fascinating book. Love it. Thanks Shannon and Andrew for sharing it".

-Hugo Sanchez

"What a wakeup call!!! OMG after 7 years in the business and I just had an eye opening experience! Thanks to the Out of the Box Owl book! I'm expanding and implementing ideas and I'm feeling like a new agent! I'm not expecting over night results but thanks to this tips I'm rolling! Just like you mentioned Mary Shannon, start living by working smarter not harder! All the little things like setting up Zillow account plus more!!! (which I didn't realize my info was not right and I lost 30 messages! I'm dying 30 leads!!!) I recommend the book not just as a reference but as a guide or yellow brick road to better yourself!!! I can't wait to put all the tools to work!!! Thank you Mary and all my owl family!!!!"

-Karla Martin

"I've only been an agent 2 years and I can use EVERYTHING in it!"   **-Sabrina Ressor**

"Awesome! The pursuit of becoming better each day is not only exciting for personal growth but also business growth and leveraging our abilities which positively affect our clients!!! Way to grow!"

-Dave Holland

"Loving the book so far..." **–Kathi Litten**

"I just started reading this book and it is so full of great content, I skimmed to page 36 and I see many areas I can use to enhance my business marketing. THANK YOU!"

-Terri Vellios

"I went to a marketing class last week and that book was talked about and was shown to us. I hope that makes you smile for my amazing state, Oklahoma!"

-Michele Breaux

"Mary Shannon Moore, I have gotten about a third of the way through your book..... it's delightfully filled with such great ideas that are so simple to implement and cost effective. Thanks so much for putting time, effort, and money into something that I'm sure is going to help me and many others. It's funny because you describe networking the way it should be done, the way that makes the most sense. However, so many of us are trying to go about it in such a suit and tie, here is my card give me yours, talk for 2 minutes kind of back and forth. Not only is your book an easy read thus far, but it's also interesting and builds motivation because I can tell myself, "Hey, I can do that."

-Tiffani Furrow

Made in the USA
Columbia, SC
18 February 2019